MEMORIES FROM AFTER THE WAR

Volume II

THE BLOOD

OF THE

PRISONERS

ALOYSIUS PAPPERT

FIRST EDITION
2016

MEMORIES FROM AFTER THE WAR
Volume II
"The Blood of the Prisoners"
by Aloysius Pappert

Translated from the author's original French language manuscript by Wolfgang Mack. IP right reserved.
English version edited by Francesca Mack
Front cover by XTOF Designs
Front cover images public domaine
Back cover image by the author

US Library of Congress Cataloging-in-Publication Data:
Library of Congress Control Number: 2016908855
ISBN-13: 978-1533091345
ISBN-10: 153309134X
BISAC: Biography and Autobiography/Personal Memoirs/
        Religion

Published by WAMFAM Press 2016
Seattle, Washington, USA

Also by the Author:
MEMORIES FROM A WAR
Volume I
"A Stolen Youth"

The Blood of the Prisoners

Dedication

My memories of my captivity as prisoner of war in Russia in the times of the Soviet Union are dedicated to all prisoners of wars any place on this earth regardless of their origins, nationalities or races and regardless of the cause for which they had fought. May they never lose hope that one day they may shake off the chains of their captivity and return safely to their home, their familes and their countries. To all the young people of the world, may they never forget that freedom is the most precious good of our life, and the love for country and our neighbors must always triumph over any hateful propaganda.

Aloysius Pappert, 2016

Foreword

"The Evil in this world is real and it never wants to die. To fight it takes courage and perseverence, and the aid of God."

This is what my long-time friend Aloysius Pappert used to say when he would tell me about his terrible years of captivity as prisoner of war in Stalin's notorious labor camps. After much thought and encouragement from his friends he now has written convincingly and with great passion about his ordeals at the hands of an inhuman system that seemed to have nothing else in mind than breaking the human spirit of its hapless prisoners. In this he shared the awful experiences of so many PoWs all over the world, no matter who they had been fighting for.

What gave him the strength to overcome hunger, sickness and the cruelty of many of his oppressors was his unshakable faith in God and the teachings of his Church. Brought up in a tight-knit Catholic family he never abandoned their high moral values. He tells movingly how he so often stepped in fearlessly to protect his fellow prisoners and to help them maintain hope when their survival was very much in doubt. When he freely confessed his Faith to his godless captors many of them reluctantly would look up to him. Even in their own evil world they understood the all-powerful force of Faith.

Aloysius Pappert's astounding talent for narrating his amazing experiences makes for fascinating reading. His unique style of writing conveys the sense of an immediacy that almost makes the reader feel that he is right there as the actions unfold.

His book is by far the best chronicle that I ever read about a pitiless time of suffering - but also about the triumph of Faith over Evil.

VICE-ADMIRAL FREDERIC MAURICE, COMMANDER OF THE FRENCH NAVY IN THE PACIFIC (RET.)

CHAPTER 1

A Journey into the Unknown

May 8, 1945. The war was over.

Our convoy of six trucks was speeding along the main highway to Zittau, away from the advancing Russians, in our frantic search of the American army to surrender to them. I had loaded what was left of my company into the two front trucks with adjutant Heiner in charge of the second truck. This way I could be in sight contact with him as we had no idea what we would encounter. The four other trucks following behind us were ordered to pick up stragglers. After half an hour I stopped the convoy to take stock.

- Have you been able to pick up some soldiers on the way?
- Oh yes, we have two trucks full.
- Are there any officers among them or men from our regiment?
- I am not sure, Lieutenant.
- Thank you, Sergeant. At the first opportunity, I'll signal to stop again so we can count them to see to which unit they belonged.

The sides of the highway were lined with burnt out tanks and trucks and with abandoned artillery and military equipment of all kinds. All this and the chaos of thousands fleeing the advancing

Russians made it difficult to move forward. I noticed a small country road that seemed to skirt Zittau. I made a sign to Heiner to follow and we stopped a little further down this road to check whether there were officers from the units of the soldiers we had picked up on the way. They all seemed totally disoriented and were hardly able to respond to our questions. A sergeant finally spoke. He and his comrades fled on May 5, their officers left their company with the idea of surrendering to the US Army.

- Have you seen other soldiers on the way?

"We stayed off the roads and cut through the fields and villages. In the last village, we learned that the end of the war was set for May 8 at midnight. Almost all the villagers were there. For two days they fed us and we were able to rest. On May 8 we hit the main road, hoping to get a ride in a truck but all vehicles were overflowing. Finally, you came by with empty trucks, a stroke of luck! The last two trucks surely picked up other soldiers."

Ten minutes later the last two trucks caught up with us. They are full of soldiers but no officers, just a warrant officer with twenty-two men and two NCOs. With Heiner we tried to establish order among them.

- I want to know the exact number of soldiers in each truck and which weapons they have. Hurry, we have to cross the border before dark.

I ask Heiner to transfer twenty soldiers to our two trucks to make a little more space in the other four vehicles. Almost every soldier had kept his assault rifle, plus we found several bazookas and hand grenades.

- We will drive at a distance of twenty yards from each other. We may meet Czech partisans on the other side of the border. Do not open fire without my order, understand? If partisans attack us we will retaliate. Since I am in the first truck, I'll give the orders. Everything will depend on how many partisans we will face and how well they are equipped. Let's go!

Our column set off into the unknown! I feared crossing this border. What a contrast to the years 1938-1939! It seemed like child's play to demolish the border posts when Germany had occupied this country, and now it was so dangerous to cross into it!

At first sight this border post seems totally abandoned. No control, not the slightest obstacle. A sign simply states 'Czechoslovakia'. Nothing else. Now we are in Czechoslovakian territory. In the distance we can hear the muffled sounds of the war on the road from Zittau to Melnik. I ask the driver to hurry. Night is falling and the road is narrow. We have to move cautiously.

We cross the first Czech village without problems. Then all of a sudden, there's a group of partisans waving us to stop.

- Slow down without stopping. If they open fire, go for it!

In the first truck, with arms ready we are set to fight back. The partisans start shooting. We respond and take to the road. The remaining partisans are routed by fire from our other trucks. Now it's clear: we are in enemy territory. It will be a matter of life and death. What to do with our weapons? We managed to cross the first holdup, but the next? If we come across more and better armed supporters our lives will count for little. I decide to stop the trucks and hear what the NCOs have to say. Nobody has the energy for a sensible analysis of the situation let alone decide one way or another. Are these men totally paralyzed by the impending danger?

"Get rid of your bazookas and hand grenades," I finally order in face of their apathy. "Throw them anywhere. Continue to drive on and pray to God that we can avoid Prague and reach Austria. If the partisans overwhelm us throw your guns and ammunition away but don't forget to render them useless!"

In the morning, at the exit of a village, a barricade of trucks blocks the road.

- Break up your weapons and throw everything away!

The Czech partisans had placed some of our Tiger tanks 200 yards down the road. Now our last hope of freedom is lost. Farewell to our "American dream". The Czechs order a few soldiers to climb down from the first two trucks and push them to a farm ahead. We hear machine gun fire and then...nothing.

The Czechs take control of the trucks and drive to another very large farm surrounded by a high wall. The buildings were empty and the yard large enough for us 400 soldiers. A commander gives the order in German for us to line up against the wall. They get their guns ready, including our famous MG-42s. There is no way to escape: they placed six machine guns, two at each end and two in the middle, and that did not even include their Kalashnikov assault rifles and some StG-44s. We are given the order to turn against the wall. In my fury with these hoodlums I scream:

- Certainly not! Let's look these murderers straight in the face!

As a reaction to my outcry one of their sharp shooters amuses himself by firing two rounds just a few inches from my head, grimacing with an expression of raw hatred. They repeat their order for us to face the wall. I stoically refuse and quite a few of my soldiers do also, but most follow the partisans' order. Some of them start to sob. I have only one thought left: to keep my self control and to die with my dignity intact. For the rest, the only thing left is to pray. So this is the way my young life is to end, in this far corner of Czechoslovakia!

They were getting their weapons ready and it is obvious these partisans are very experienced men. The machine guns on my right are starting to fire into the lineup. Several of our soldiers collapse.

Just then an armored car comes crashing through the farm gate. Russian soldiers emerge, firing in the air and disarm the Czechs. A Russian general leads the operation from his armored car. The massacre is stopped. These Russians who failed to kill me at Hermannstadt come out of nowhere to save my life. The absurdity of war!

Before leaving the farm I take a last look at our dead and the wounded lying against the wall. No time for pity or to collect them. The Russians have already pushed us out and are herding us into trucks. We have changed masters.

The Russian soldiers who guard us look us over.

- Uri-Uri? One of them asks by tapping on his watch.

I understand and I tell my men to give their watches to the soldier. I had two: the one on my wrist I hand over like everyone else, and another, hidden on me. With a happy grin one of the Russians shows his stash overflowing with pocket watches.

- Your spoils of war, I say to him in German.

- Yes, I have already quite a few he replied in an almost perfect German. I knew that in Russia, German was taught in school.

I ask permission to get something to drink. We had not had a drop of water for twenty-four hours.

News about our arrival must have been spreading fast because when our convoy arrives in the next village, the locals come to meet us with buckets full of water. We were finally able to drink and fill our water bottles. The attitude of the villagers showed how frightened they were of the Russians. We resumed our journey into the unknown.

Soon we see a sign: Prague 50 miles. On the sides of the road, piles of military equipment and huge columns of prisoners walking to nowhere, dazed and haggard. The sad remains of the 'Thousand Year German Empire' is dragging itself in rags through this remote corner of Czechoslovakia. We, at least, are riding in trucks.

Now we are prisoners of the Russians, the very fate we had been trying so hard to avoid.

What kind of life would we be facing as their POWs?

*

The Blood of the Prisoners

CHAPTER 2

The bitter Taste of being a Prisoner

Reaching the outskirts of Prague we find out that now we are prisoners of the new Czech army and we have to obey their orders. First the partisans, then the Russians and now the Czech army. We no longer have control over our destiny, we are a herd that the winners are trading as they like and deal with as they wish. Woe to the vanquished!

Our new masters do not dally with their new unchecked power they hold over us. They chase us down from the trucks with rifle butts and under constant shouting they make us join two to three thousand other prisoners. They force our ragged masses into a march at a pace that is more running than marching. The younger ones can keep pace but the legs of the older Home Guard men cannot, and they are falling behind. The Czech soldiers push them ahead and beat them to make them stay with our column. Those who cannot are simply shot on the spot. A truck picks up the dead bodies.

While marching ahead I scan this haggard mass of humanity in the hope of recognizing some soldiers from my company, but in vain, not a single familiar face. Suddenly our column is stopped.

We must line up on the sidewalk to let a car pass, some kind of jeep with an officer on board, maybe of the new Czech army He speaks to us in German: we will go to a big soccer stadium where we will stay until further notice. There will be no walking or talking among prisoners. Upon arrival there each prisoner will receive some bread.

Taking advantage of this pause I keep trying to recognize a face. I could see very few officers and NCOs, but still no one I know. My camouflage jacket made me look like any soldier. I thought of what it disguised, my lieutenant's uniform, my pistol with two full magazines, my compass and my map. These would be my last chance to escape but would also mean certain death if they were to be discovered.

*

Half an hour later we enter the stadium. As promised, they give us a piece of bread. A mass of prisoners is already crammed in there, lying on the ground, one on top of each other. I tried as much as possible to stay with the new arrivals while seeking a place for me that would pass quickly into the shade when the arena would turn into furnace - the sun was already starting to beat down on us. The last prisoners being herded in could not find a space for themselves. A loudspeaker ordered everyone to lie down. All movements that the guards would deem dangerous would immediately be punished.

I am lying on my stomach keeping my pistol to my side. The piece of bread and water had cut my hunger a little. I fell asleep. Three shots and brutal screaming pulled me from my sleep. One of the injured tried to straighten himself, shouting: "You bastards! You murderers!" Immediately several shots rang out from different points which silenced him permanently. The prisoners that had arrived before us were wounded soldiers that had been taken from their hospitals in Prague when the new Czech army took power. It was rumored that the seriously injured had been evacuated by train to Germany. What could one believe here?

The day seemed endless. Everyone did his needs without leaving his place, lying down as ordered. Ten yards from me a soldier knelt to urinate. A shot in the head - he died instantly.

The last weeks of the war parade in front of me in my mind, in disjointed images. First, the figure of Marshal Schörner came up. They said he was a model grandfather with perfect manners but behind this facade were barbaric impulses that made him hang his own soldiers. When I had met him by chance on the road he was actually still a general but already wore his Marshal's uniform. According to Colonel Hausenberger, he did not even wait until his appointment as Field Marshal had been made official and already he was throwing his weight around, getting rid of many of his detractors. This behavior was characteristic of the Nazi leaders who were always looking for ways to satisfy their outsized ambitions. But today he is far away, far from languishing in his own shit in the middle of his brothers in arms!

I had already been a prisoner once, in Italy, in early June 1944. How foolish of me to have escaped from my American captors thinking that the war would be over anyway at the end of the year. What a jerk! What an absolute idiot I had been! Apparently I said these words aloud because my neighbor asked me why. I turned my back without replying. What's the point ? I preferred to let the past stay inside me, I had no desire to share it with anyone. I relived the day of July 20 in Aschaffenburg. I thought about the attack against Hitler. So many questions to be asked about that fiasco which cost the lives of thousands of soldiers and civilians, some shot or hanged, until April 1945! I came to the conclusion that this attack could not have succeeded without the help of the Allied. But nothing like this had occurred. I remembered that at that time the Allied had demanded a unconditional surrender of Nazi Germany. They did not want to have to negotiate with Germany but us Germans would have gotten rid of Hitler all by ourselves. Too bad for all those Germans who had never belonged to the regime and wanted to keep their faith in a new Germany, the Germany of Goethe, Lessing and Kant, who would have been worthy of being received into the family of free nations. My remembrances, my questioning and my dreams and my wishful thinking were suddenly interrupted by the loud speaker who gave the order to leave.

*

It was late afternoon. We left the stadium in columns of 500 to 1000 prisoners, but many did not get up. For us survivors a new forced march began towards Prague. I stayed in the middle of our column and I realized we were heading to the suburbs rather than the center of the city. We arrived at a suburb that had not suffered too much from the battles for the liberation of the city. We walked along beautiful houses with flower gardens. One could guess the faces behind the windows. For two weeks they had seen German soldiers passing by fleeing Prague, and now how many herds of prisoners like us?

The street was cleared of civilians. We sat on one side of the street, the Czechs stood opposite. The Czech commander talked with a Russian officer and it was obviously not a contest of politeness! It seemed that the Russian gave the Czech a dressing down. The Czech hardly replied, merely repeating "Da, da." What were they saying? Was it that the Soviets' instructions had not been followed correctly? How could we know? A car comes by and tells us to remain there until further notice. We are exhausted, without a drop of water. You could read an immense despair in the eyes of the older ones who were undoubtedly thinking of their children and even grandchildren. They had no news of them for weeks, months.

When the Czech captain drove by me me I stood up and asked if we could have some water. He barely gave me a look and motioned to his driver to continue. But behind me a woman's voice whispers from the shadows of a tree in German:

- You certainly must be thirsty. I'll see what I can do.

She soon returns with other women coming out of the gardens with buckets full of water. As soon as the Czech soldiers see them they shout and shoot into the air.

- Leave quickly. They can kill you!

They leave the buckets of water behind us and run away. It was getting dark and fortunately the road is poorly lit. Everything happens very quickly, the guards saw nothing. But alerted by the gunfire the captain returns in his jeep and demands explanations from his men. He grabs a loudspeaker apparently shouting orders or making threats. All the lights the windows of houses go out.

My companions are calling me to let them drink. It was not the right time, our guards' eyes were on us. An hour later as we were lying on the pavement, I organized a distribution of water as silently as possible. On the opposite sidewalk the Czechs were sleeping more or less like us. Freshened, I look at my watch: almost midnight. I close my eyes with a final thought for my mother and these women who had risked their lives to help us. For them we were not enemies but unfortunate prisoners with an uncertain future. I still had my rosary with the Lady medal in my threadbare military pouch, one last thought of my mother. These little personal items give me a sense of peace and protection.

*

We were rudely awakened. The day is not yet risen. The Czech soldiers push us unceremoniously to go again, faster, faster. We cut through small gardens, and out of breath come out on a main road with tall buildings on each side. A boulevard was rendered impassable in parts by remnants of barricades, blocks of collapsed walls and houses burned to a rubble. The evidence from the terrible fighting tell us to face the obvious: no hope for mercy from the Czech. They will not forget any time soon their sufferings during the German occupation and the price they paid for their freedom.

At day break we join another column of prisoners ahead of us. Many of them are injured, especially those among the last of their column. I approached a group of officers. All have been very injured in the battles of February and March 1945 and hospitalized in Prague. In late April a part of them was able to leave the city towards Austria. But then new casualties arrived and were piled on top them in their hospitals. Why weren't those evacuated, maimed as they were? A major with a strong Austrian accent explained it to me:

- We were in a hospital outside the city and we experienced the battle of Prague without participating in it. We had German and Czech doctors. Of course we thought about our situation and our future. Only two days ago the Czechs have kicked us out of our hospital and left us in a vacant lot under the supervision of the Czech militia.

- You were serving in what unit?

- In the Army Centre Corps, under the command of Marshal Schörner.

- Me too.

- Ah yes? But you look so young.

- Yes, but I am a lieutenant since January 1945 and I ended the war on May 8 in Germany, 15 miles from Zittau with what was left of our battalion, just twenty men.

- So under your camouflage jacket hides an officer? What age?

- 20 years.

- So you do not know about the last battles in Czechoslovakia?

- No. All I know is that the famous 'executioner of Hitler' abandoned his army on May 3 to save his skin. When I think of all the soldiers he hanged as 'traitors' I have only one wish: that the Czech resistance finds him and make him suffer the same fate!

Silence. An officer asked me if I saw, with my own eyes, what I am talking about. And how ! In short, I tell them the story of my meeting with Schörner.

- It was true, sighs the officer. We had heard of these cases from a major of the 78th Infantry Division.

- Where is he, now, this major?

- We met him two days ago, but since then, no more contact.

- Was it perhaps major Reinhard? Maybe I could find him.

While walking, I continued to hear more about the last days of the war. I learned that the Red Army had arrived in Prague the evening of May 8 and had fought a fierce battle in the center of Prague against the last German troops, mainly SS soldiers. It was the Vlassov army made up of White Russians who had fought against the Soviets, first in Russia and then on the Western front wearing the uniform of the Waffen-SS. In 1945, before the liberation of Prague, the remnants of the Vlasov army arrived in Czechoslovakia to fight against the Red Army while trying to reach Austria. Everything was finished on May 11, three days after the surrender.

Some of the seriously injured had great difficulties keeping up the pace. I asked several young soldiers to help them because in the back the Czechs kept on killing those who could no longer walk. With an NCO at my side we helped the Austrian major along. At first he did not want to hear about it but then he came around to accept and we thus we could stay with our column.

- We will arrive soon on the Charles Bridge, said the major. This is the most beautiful and best known bridge in Prague.

- What is the name the river that flows under this bridge?

- This is the Moldau.

- Did you know Prague before the war?

-You know I'm 56, I was in the first war in the army of the Austrian Empire and later I often visited Prague and Budapest, two fascinating cities.

Thinking of the past his eyes lit up with an expression of intense happiness as if he did no longer belong to this world. We were in the middle of the Charles Bridge when he asked me point-blank:

- Are you a believer?

- Yes I am.

- So help me to get close to the railing when the next Czech guard is far enough so that he will not notice anything.

Once there he said: "Now let me go! And God bless you!" Then, in a superhuman effort, he jumped onto the railing and shouted out loud: "Long live my beloved fatherland, viva Austria" and threw himself into the Moldau.

I quickly melded back into the column and went up several rows. Behind us gunfire erupted. Who were they shooting? I did not try to find out. That unhappy major chose death freely because with a prosthesis of a leg he could have no illusions about his chances to survive as a prisoner of war. May God grant him eternal peace. He was 56 years old but I, who was barely 20, I did not want to die. I wanted to see my parents again.

This desperate act of bravery and desparation had infuriated the Czechs who slaughtered again and again all those who could not keep up the pace of this forced march. Not the time to fall back. I continued to move up the column to the middle. Just then some trucks with Russian soldiers arrived.

Another change of masters.

*

CHAPTER 3

Learning the Fate of the POWs

I estimated that about 5,000 prisoners were leaving Prague in the morning, escorted by the Red Army.

Our first stop took us into a make-shift camp fences of barbed wire and floodlights. Lot of prisoners must have already passed through there judging from the garbage all over the field. Our guards gave us a piece of bread and water. Late May, the temperature was mild. This was not the abomination of our first internment in that stadium. We are allowed to move around but I still cannot find anyone from my unit.

About ten o'clock the Russians announced that tomorrow our group will leave this camp and walk in the direction of Brno, about a sixty miles from Prague. There we can expect regular trains that will lead us into Austria where we will be handed over to the US Army who will demobilize us and send us home.

I told myself to remain skeptical. This beautiful speech in impeccable German somehow rang false in my ears. I had trouble believing in such a happy ending. Others let their joy be known.

Most prisoners were already calculating the date of their return home.

Very early the next day we start on our march to Brno. Before leaving the camp we get two pieces of bread and some water. At least the Russians are not making us starve. I had no idea that we would have nothing else to put our teeth on until Brno. Look! Our guards have changed. These new ones look mean and aggressive, with their fingers on the trigger of their Kalashnikovs. We would see a lot more of these brutes.

Our long column of prisoners was moving along on a road parallel to the highway. I still could not find a familiar face. Feeling alone in the middle of these 5000 people is more oppressive than solitude, you are overcome by a haunting feeling of vulnerability. Suddenly, I think I hear a familiar dialect. I make my way closer to two soldiers. The first is from Neuhof near Fulda, the other from Marbach, between Fulda and Hünfeld. Comrades from my home area! This is heart-warming. The first is Otto Fischer, a sergeant, 26 years old. He worked as a bookkeeper in household supply shop in Fulda. At 19, he was drafted into the Wehrmacht, and after two years in Denmark he was sent to the Russian front. Wounded in 1943 he was sent to Fulda to recover. Then, after three months of intensive training at Wildflecken, was promoted to NCO and joined his division early 1944 near Kiev. Somehow he wound up as prisoner in our column. His companion, Karl Schmitt is a corporal, 27, wounded several times. He worked at his father's large farm in Marbach. He is very friendly and reminds me of my unfortunate Corporal Schneider. Talkative but very attentive to his surroundings. Then I introduce myself with my rank and military past. There will be time for them to ask questions later.

First a long day's walking. Around noon we are given an hour's rest. I want to tell my new friends my intention to escape and to try to reach the Americans. They are flabbergasted. What's wrong with you? For them the escape attempt is nonsense, foolishness. In Brno, they said we will board comfortable trains towards Austria, go to the Americans for demobilization and for our return home. Haven't you heard the good news last night or what? I hesitated to tell them what was in the back of my mind. Just like most they had noticed the change of guards the day before, or if they had not, like Karl, they did not see what to me was very clear. But there is nothing you can do when a misplaced confidence blinds their minds. I knew that without accomplices my escape plan would be unrealistic. Since those two had refused my proposal I had to get rid of my revolver, my compass and my road map as soon as possible. With Karl in tow we headed toward the woods. Many prisoners, no one is looking. I left everything in a thicket, revolver, magazines, compass, map, and my freedom. "My dear Karl, I tell you the dream to get back to our homeland is over!" I took a bite of my bread and drank a few sips of water. The other two followed suit. And we resumed our march towards Brno.

- Otto, what day is it?

- Pentecost Sunday. When I was little we always were on a pilgrimage to the monastery of Fulda Frauenberg to attend high mass. After that the Nazis drove the Franciscan monks out and installed a Waffen-SS school in their abbey. I hope the Franciscans will return, at least those who are still alive.

- God willing, we shall know one day.

At sunset, a stop in a meadow with a small stream and we take the opportunity to fill our water bottles. Before nightfall our guards divided us into four squares and stationed themselves around us. We are a flock of sheep, they are the sheepdogs. The other guards settled near trucks for a night of dining and drinking. Soon we hear them sing and we distinguish the voices of women. I was hungry but all I had was a few sips of water, preferring to save the little bread that was left for the next day.

Dawn was breaking. Our guards sounded the start of the day. Change of pace, forced march! Around noon a little break and again we leave in quick time. "The trains are waiting for us, they should not leave without us!" I had said that half-ironically to my companions. "It's certain"! Otto replied, totally missing my point:

"I look forward to being at home!" Karl and I have no comment. The evening dusk, with the identical program: a meadow, a small stream.

On Whit Monday the same furious pace. The oldest and weakest start to fall behind. The guards bring up the rear by jostling and barking but not for long. Already the first shots ring out and laggards are collapsing. The Russians rob them, take their uniforms and throw the corpse on the side. You should have seen the stragglers use their last strength to catch up with the group! "Sink or Swim", this is not a figure of speech but a reality. The unfortunate murdered in cold blood! Impossible to count them now. Bursts of machine guns goad us ahead in our forced march. I will never forget this terrible Whit Monday.

Again in the evening, on an empty stomach, we are preparing to spend another night in a meadow, very green and flowery. How if we make ourselves a good soup? We pick dandelions and other fragrant herbs that I know, while Otto and Karl light a small fire to cook the broth in our bowls. It was not anything of substance, but it was hot and we all swallowed it happily. We were alive and wanted to remain so.

*

On the third day, back to walking as normal. We were supposed not to be far from Brno. In the late afternoon our column halted. We are six miles from our destination. There are two large camps for something like 20,000 prisoners. We enter the first of the camps and receive water and a large piece of dry bread.

- Let's stay together, the way to Russia will be long.
- Towards Russia?
- Yes, Otto, but our 'comfortable trains' will be cattle cars. And tomorrow or the day after tomorrow we will be taken on these trains.
- I thought so, said Karl.
- Stay here, I'll try to find out more.

I saw a group of officers in discussion. I approach. These men had fled before the Red Army in the hope of getting to Austria to surrender to the Americans. I take a lieutenant aside and he says:

"In March my Panzer Division was in eastern Czechoslovakia fighting back against the Red Army. There have been huge losses in men and material, resulting in the rest of the division coming under the command of Marshal Schörner. In early May we realized that the only way to escape the Russians was to surrender. With three trucks and handguns we managed to join the US Army. We gave them our weapons and they directed us to a camp where we were very well received. An officer asked us where we came from in Germany. A major gave him all the details. The superior to whom the officer made his report had a strange reaction: he laughed heartily. We did not have time to ask why, but he immediately ordered to serve us coke plus a pack of cigarettes, adding: "Go then to the canteen!" The American cigarettes and Coca-Cola were already quite a discovery! The canteen was a large tent where they gave us white bread and corned beef - still a novelty - and again Coca-Cola. A real treat! We said long live America and freedom!"

His story made my mouth water.

"There is more ... The next morning coffee, white bread, jam, all as much as we could eat. Overnight other prisoners arrived and the camp was full. Before noon several American officers showed up and we learned that in the evening we would leave the camp to a new destination. "Good luck!" And he turned around. Then our major caught up with him and asked in English: "General, what destination?" The other replied but we found out later: "You will be handed to the Russians. I'm sorry, this is an agreement between President Roosevelt and Stalin: the US Army agreed to hand over all German prisoners of war to the Red Army and all civilian prisoners. This does not apply to the English army! Don't tell your other officers. They will find out soon enough." He saluted and left. We asked the major what he had said: "I'll explain later." In the evening, we eventually were led out of the camp and

then the sky fell in! What a welcoming committee! "Dawai! Dawai! quick! quick!" we heard the Russians yelling! They put us in trucks, Kalashnikov butts into our backs and after driving all night we arrived in the morning at this camp. Freedom lasted only a moment! At least it felt good for a while!"

Looking me over the lieutenant said we probably were the same age, perhaps with the same education?

- Good road to hell! God bless you.
- You too.

What a story! Like so many others we had risked our lives racing through Czechoslovakia without realizing that we would wind up a commodity for the victors to share. It only remained for me to find Karl and Otto back in Camp 1. But their camp was already empty, all the prisoners transferred elsewhere. No time to find out about them, we had to go quickly join our column, forced on by the guards "Dawai! Dawai!" In no time this word had a taken a haunting place in our lives!

The night that followed was marked by lots of anxiety and nightmares. Only a long prayer enabled me to sleep.

*

CHAPTER 4

On a Death Train to Nowhere

The sun was beating down hard when I woke up. Around me a mass of bodies, some still slumped in sleep, others tottering to wake up. For breakfast I took a sip of warm water and immediately an overwhelming feeling of tiredness overcame me, a terrifying mixture of physical exhaustion and moral dejection. In this state of despair I had only one wish - to die. Yes, finish it already, stop the fight. But then a voice whispered to me: "I am always with you." Somehow I felt reborn. My mind once more wants me to live. I knelt, clasped my hands: "Hail Mary ..." No! I do not want to die in this wretched camp!

When I see the lieutenant I had spoken with the day before I signal to him to come to my place as there is a small space on my side. He pushes his way through and tells me that we shall leave tonight. Four trains with five thousand of us on each train, more cars for guards, a hundred prisoners in each car under the responsibility of an officer. His name is Helmut. We are both born in 1924, he in January, me at the end of the year. He had been a student up to 19 followed by the usual months of para-military training before being drafted into the army where he rose to lieutenant. Then he joined a tank regiment and was sent to eastern Czechoslovakia in late 1944.

- And what was your military time like?

I remembered the mule driver during my Italian campaign who we had nicknamed 'old' when he was just was 25! We were now premature veterans trying to make it to 21 or what was left of our youth.

"I am a product of Berlin, born and raised in Berlin. My father was a professor of cardiology in the best clinic in Berlin. Originally he was a partner with another cardiologist. My mother was a housewife. We had a big house in an upper middle-class neighborhood. I had two brothers, four and six years older. One was reported missing in Stalingrad, the other died in 1943 near Minsk. Last year my father's clinic was bombed in a night raid and completely destroyed. Many died there. He was the sole owner since his Jewish partner had gone to America in '38. After the clinic bombing my father opened a cardiology practice and general medicine in our home and my mother became his assistant. The last time I had them on the phone, my father told me they were going to leave Berlin for Bavaria. After that no more news. And you?"

I described my military career from March 1942. At the end he told me:

- You have really lived through just about the entire war to its end. Had you volunteered?

- You know, Helmut, there are worlds between us. I am a country boy and you grew up in the capital. I did not volunteer nor am I a Nazi sympathizer. I hated those people. In my life as a soldier I was always guided by my father's advise. He always told me that I will be a good soldier because I think of the lives of my comrades and of our Ten Commandments. He also told me that no one knew where and how the war would end, but my faith in God and my prayers would help me overcome the worst, and eventually return home.

I showed him my cross and the medal of the Virgin and also my wallet with some photos and personal memories.

"I, too, am a Christian but Protestant. Originally, my parents were not very religious but became so around 1943, after losing two sons. Hitler's madness and his phantasy of the 'Thousand Year Reich' had turned them anti-Nazi! Anyway my father had never been a great admirer of Hitler. But then, just like his former partner, they were officers in the First World War. Hitler had impressed them because he had promised to free Germany from poverty and to make the the German people proud again. When even experienced people like they could be persuaded by Hitler's follies, do you think that we young ones could understand what was happening? I remember for example the beginnings of the SA who marched through Berlin almost every day. They fought against the communists and the anarchists. Constantly there were parades. One day when I was 9 I went home singing the Horst-Wessel song. My father asked me if I knew what I was singing. Not really. Then he explained the exact meaning of words by saying that in this song the 'reactionaries' who were to be shot were people like us because in their minds the word 'reactionary' simply meant people who respected the national order prior to the Nazi revolution. He made a comparison with the French Revolution, when an opponent at the time was anyone who did not submit to the dictate of the Revolution. Today it's the same in Germany, their targets are the democratic parties and the priests. Taking my hands my father had told me not tell anyone about this conversation. The succeeding events surely showed he was right."

We continued exchanging our childhood memories, our feasts and our dreams and forgot our empty stomach, quenching our tyrannical thirst with small sips of lukewarm water. As I had always taken care of my watch I knew it was about 5pm when we were to depart. After us the camp would be filled again with 20,000 new prisoners.

*

A first column of 5000 prisoners left the camp. We waited our turn. A Russian who spoke perfect German ordered us to form rows of ten and thus 500 rows. An officer among the prisoners would be responsible for ten rows to fill a rail car. I told Helmut to try to put us in neighboring cars. Then we said goodbye and God speed!

Helmut walked away with his hundred men. I gathered mine in rows of five, one behind the other, explaining to them that this would facilitate the counting. I present them to the three Russians guarding us and after a military salute declare that our column is ready to embark. This little display of discipline impresses them. We head to our car without being recounted. Before boarding we fill our water bottles and each of us gets a piece of bread. As soon as we are inside the Russians close the door.

We find out quickly that we would not have enough room for all of us to lie down. I called for attention:

"We all know you are thirsty and hungry. Drink a little of your water and eat some of your bread. I do not think we'll get anything else for the next few days. I am in charge of this car. It's my duty to help and protect you. I was awarded the Iron Cross 1st class for saving the lives of many of my fellow soldiers and believe me, in the coming months, we will need all the courage we can muster and with Gods help we may live to find the way to freedom and to our families. Nazism is over. I do not know if you are believers but we Germans will have to return to the path of prayer in order to find the strength to forget the Nazi horror. All of us, both we here in this prisoner train and our loved ones living in their bombed out cities will be held accountable for Hitler's crimes. Germany will be ostracized by all other nations and for a long time. To start our life as prisoners of war I ask you to join me in a little prayer even if you've lost your faith."

Many followed me in my prayer or at least listened in silence.

- Now everyone finds a place. There is not enough for everyone to lie down. So some will be sitting, some lying down. The night will be long. I will stay by the door.

It was warm and soon getting hot. Jackets were quickly shed and rolled into balls to serve as pillows.

*

Three days later, a foul stench had filled every corner of the wagon.

- Lieutenant, come see, I believe this one is dead!

I forced my way to the other side of the car. It was true. All I could do was to make a cross on the forehead of this unfortunate fellow: "May God grant you eternal peace." I asked the two soldiers who had joined me fervently in my prayers to sit next to me at the door.

The following day four more deaths, followed by the same ceremony, the same prayer. A sergeant asked me if I considered it useful to keep half their nameplates. How should I know? I replied that there would certainly be a moment when the train would stop and we could ask the Russians. We had no clue what was to happen to us. But I was touched by the attention the man had given to this matter and I thanked him.

On the fifth day, six more soldiers lay dead. The stench was becoming excruciating. I could read real terror rising in the eyes of the prisoners. The slightest panic in such close quarters would have wreaked havoc. It was absolutely necessary that I took control over these men to give them a purpose, to channel their minds to battle a rising madness.

- We will consolidate the dead near the door and we'll scream with all our strength to attract the attention of our guards!

This helped the men to violently shout out their anguish. It also made the train slow down. Minutes after these screams of hunted animals the convoy stops, the door opens. Three Russians pointing their Kalashnikovs at us. The officer ordered me to step down while a soldier locks the car behind me. Why did we scream? I quickly tell him the situation: eleven dead, the furnace heat, the stench caused by feces and the corpses, nothing to drink ... At this rate, none of us will remain alive.

- As we are not yet in Russia, it is not possible to stop the train. But late in the afternoon we will be in an open field near a river and there you will get rid of the bodies. No need to keep an identity document for the deaths. Our health services will do that.

- Can the door be left open for some air?

- Granted, but be aware that you are responsible. Any attempt to escape will be punished by death.

The door of the car was wide open. The officer immediately stepped back when the stench hit him. He said something in Russian that made the two soldiers laugh. A quick look toward Helmut's car. I saw that his door was open, but he could not get off.

The train left. The open door and the fresh air was an incredible relief. I again spoke to the group, repeated what the Russians had told me, trying to instill some hope and courage. At the next stop we could drop our dead ourselves and the medical service of the Red Army would take care of their burial and register their names so that they can be gathered later in a German prisoners of war cemetery. Late in the afternoon we would receive water and food and I was hoping we could clean the car. As for that, I probably was led by hope but it seemed to me that it would be possible to have a sensible discussion with the Russian officer.

Indeed, late in the afternoon the train stopped. The officer appeared before our wagon, two soldiers holding us at gunpoint. I immediately offered to start lowering the dead with a system that would satisfy the Russians: two men would lower one dead onto the ground and then immediately go back into the car. While twenty-two prisoners executed my orders to the letter I continued to talk with the officer and made a request: let the other eighty-five prisoners go to the river to wash while a NCO would remain in the car with three men to clean it. Maybe we could get one or two buckets of chlorine to disinfect? The officer hesitated. After all we represented the invaders who brought death and widespread ruin throughout the Soviet Union. At all costs I had to find the right words.

- I personally take full responsibility for eighty-five men and the NCO with the three men who will clean the car.

Finally, he agreed to give me two buckets of water. Nothing more. Then the NCO comes down from the car. Without hesitation, he told me that he will need to recover two or three coats from the dead to wash the car. The Russian officer agrees. Another question: "Will we have water and food?"

- No, you will have to return into you car. Do not drink water from the river, it is not clean.

- How many more days do we travel?

- Four days.

- And you're still with us?

- No. I leave the convoy tomorrow.

So in a spontaneous gesture I gave him my decoration, the famous Iron Cross 1st class. He kissed it saying it would be a memory of a German officer he would not forget. He shook my hand and walked away. Only much later did I understand what made Russian officers who had finished the war on German territories different.

Through the discipline of my soldiers all occupants of our car could wash in the small river in rows of five and return to the car in order. The occupants of Helmut's car did the same. But there was disorder somewhere. Gunfire erupted and the Russians began to scream: "Dawai! Dawai!" Pushing everyone. An unending counting of prisoners ensued. As all soldiers in my wagon were back in place in perfect discipline we received half a bottle of fresh water and a serving of peas.

Our car had been cleaned but the smell had not disappeared entirely, it permeated everything. The Russian officer let us keep the two water buckets which now serve as toilets for the rest of the trip. The sliding door was not locked, I could keep it open for some air. But at nightfall the door was again tightly closed leaving us in a claustophobic heat.

The next morning the train stops at a small station. From the open door I see the officer with whom we had worked. An hour later the convoy leaves without him.

Having fresh air coming into the car made the stench a little more bearable. I advised the men to conserve water and food and to to take a small portion of dry peas, chewing them long to salivate and not swallow until they had everything reduced to a fine pulp. In this way it was more likely to cut the hunger. But despite these recommendations, on the second day, the majority of men had drunk their water and finished their pea ration. Alas, at this slow pace and in this heat the dying would resume, especially as the door was closed again.

I tried to organize some kind of meeting with three NCOs to share with them my fears. There was not much we could do other than a plan to block the door if the opportunity arose. At the end of the second day several prisoners showed extreme signs of weakness. In the night the heat was suffocating and the stench nauseating. Not a breath of fresh air. Most of the men were shirtless, drenched, pouring sweat.

On the morning of the third day I asked everyone to show their presence by raising his arm. Not all raised theirs. Accompanied by my NCOs, we inspected the car. Five men had not survived the night and at least six others were dying. Then, as on the first time we yelled with all our strength. The train moved very slowly and then stopped for an hour.

The sliding door opens, three Russian soldiers face me. I want to step out but their Kalashnikovs pointing at me quickly make me change my mind. I realize that to our guards we are nothing but some form of livestock and our keepers could care less about our state of mind. I try to make them understand that we have several dead in our car. They do not understand anything. So I spread the fingers of one hand to mimic the number 5 and saying, "Kaput! Kaput!" One of the guards finally got the idea and pulled me out of the car together with the NCO. With his finger the Russian points to the dead and said: "Dawai! Dawai!" motioning to throw them out. We descend the but he threatens us and makes us understand that we must discard the dead right at the edge of the track, nothing else. Our work done we are chased back to the car with rifle butts in our kidneys, "Dawai! Dawai!" The door immediately closed, the train departed at the speed of an old hearse.

Our last drops of water did not help. The thirst became unbearable. Most of the prisoners looked at me in absolute dejection. What to do to help them? I racked my brains but my experience told me that with these morons of guards there was no hope. There was only prayer, always the last resort. The train started rolling a little faster and I started:

"Comrades, let us not give up hope. Let us pray together. God will never abandon us."

I pray in a loud voice and to my surprise, several of my men start to pray with me, although feebly, totally exhausted.

The night had become a little cooler, perhaps there was a little rain. I made the tour with my NCOs: seven more had died during the night, and three more were on the verge.

Next evening the train suddenly stops. The door opened wide. One of my men stands up and starts to run out of the car. A shower of bullets end his life. These same brutal guards from yesterday again point to our dead and motion us to lower them down to the side of the tracks.

Since our departure from Bruno we have lost twenty five of our soldiers.

The door stays wide open, but we do not dare to go outside. A little later an officer wearing different shoulder pads tell us that the train would arrive tomorrow at noon in the Donbass region. Before that there would be a last stop to get rid of the dead and we would receive a portion of fresh water.

- And today, no water?
- No, there is none.
- Can we empty our buckets?
- Go for it.

Two able bodied men go out and empty the buckets while I am asking the officer if we can leave the door open. He hesitates, asks the guards' opinion and finally allows us a small opening until evening. What happiness!

Last night in this coffin on rails I dreamed of hell, the devil brandishing a Kalashnikov. And always these screams: Dawai-Dawai-Dawai! The heat was excruciating. I woke up, sticky with sweat. Dawn was breaking. Around me men collapsed ready to die. What time was it ? I forgot to wind my watch but so what? Like for the watch, the time of life also had stopped.

The train slows down and after a long screech comes to rest in the open field. I open the door of the car take in a morning breath of fresh air. With the sergeant and two soldiers, we immediately block the door to prevent any suicide attempts. But nobody moves. I then approached each of them for an encouraging word, force a small smile. Five soldiers do not respond. I shake them: nothing. I feel their pulse: nothing. End of the trip for them! We move their bodies near the door. This morning I would like to accompany them with a final prayer. I am about to make the sign of the cross on their foreheads when a guard stopped me, yapping I don't know what orders, firing in the air. At first bewildered and then unable to restrain myself I scream at him: "Shut up! You bastard!" And with the help of a NCO, we lay the corpses at his feet. Surprised, he jumped back, petrified! Another guard comes. They take the bodies away.

*

Other Russian soldiers distribute water in each car. I jump off the car wanting to finish the blessing of my five comrades, praying to God to grant them eternal peace. I plant myself in front of the three guards by making the sign of the cross. They do not move. An inner voice told me not to be afraid to show my faith. These devils back down not knowing what to do. I go back in the car. The sergeant, the corporal and the soldiers stare at me as if I was coming back from Mars. Suddenly we hear new screams, shots, the guards buckle the door of our car. The train is leaving, and we have not had a drop of water.

*

It really took a lot of courage not to succumb to our agonies. But I was not the only one struggling. Towards the end of the trip, one of my soldiers approaches me. He wants to talk to me but the noise of the train makes it difficult to talk. He sits down beside me. He is 22, his father was a high Nazi official and his entire family was wiped out in the latest bombing of Magdeburg. Enlisted in the Home Guard he was shipped out in the beginning of April to Czechoslovakia. He had not even had the opportunity to fire a single shot before being captured by the Red Army. He made the march from Prague to Brno and here he is on this train:

"Lieutenant, I have observed you since we left Brno. You seem to be able to master all situations and you always find a word to give us courage. I understand why. This is because you are a believer. You prayed for us and there are comrades who have prayed with you. I was ashamed because I don't know how to pray. My parents did not practice any religion. My sister, who also died in the bombing of Magdeburg, unfortunately, got to know that 'Providence' of Hitler. I understood that faith in God makes you happy and helps in the difficulties of life."

- What is your first name ?
- Thorsten.
- Thorsten, your name is very popular in eastern Germany. Listen, I'll tell you my encounter with another Thorsten. He was an SS captain and then I met an SS colonel.

I told them my story on how I came to know these men and how they had turned away from being Nazis. He listened together with my sergeant and some others. When I had finished, all looked at me with a certain awe.

- Faith can move mountains, Thorsten. You see, life without faith in God is a troubled life without end. Believe me, many of us will never see our homeland again, our families, our friends, but faith and prayer may give you the strength to resist dispair.

- What should I do to believe? I do not know how to pray!

I was exhausted, disarmed by this question, the most difficult of all.

- Thorsten, simply ask God to show you the way to become his servant and help your comrades in all circumstances. This will be the start of a new life for you. Try to stay with me tomorrow and the days to come.

Hunger and thirst have taken possession of my whole being. I was not able to say a word or even think. I fell deeply asleep, like being in a dark cave. When I woke up, the train slowed, the deafening noise of the rails became softer.

I got up to wish everyone a good day:

- A new day begins, another gift from our Lord Jesus Christ. Also thank the Blessed Virgin, for she will protect us throughout our life and especially here as a prisoner of war.

I recited aloud a Hail Mary. With my swollen and cracked lips, my parched tongue, I still went through this prayer. In the half-light I noticed that the majority of men listened to me. Then the most painful daily ritual: making the round with my NCO among the living and finding who had died. We visited each row, shook those who were still asleep and found those who would not awaken any more. Seven more soldiers dead! We deposited their corpses near the door.

No time to pray for their salvation. The train suddenly stops, the door is pulled open. Our three guards are there, this time they do not shout at us. I get out of the car followed by the sergeant and we lower the seven dead soldiers, one by one. We line them up in front of our door with a last prayer, and then get back into our car. Throughout the ceremony the guards did not make a move. I make them understand that we want the the door slightly open. They accept, and I thank them with a gesture. One of them replied: "Da, da." Glancing toward Helmut's car I do not see anyone. Our train departs and arrives at our destination in the afternoon.

The sound of thunder announced a storm. Rain would be welcome, it would mean happiness!

*

CHAPTER 5

Thus starts my Life as a Prisoner

The train pulled into the station in pouring rain. For us this was a true blessing! You should have seen us clamber out of our train cars as fast as we could, hands cupped together to catch as much rain water as possible for our parched throats. In front of us we could see small wooden houses clustered around what seemed to be coal mines. Our uniforms were soaked but we relished every moment of it. Two prisoners could not be part of this 'resurrection'. They had not moved when we scrambled out of our car. Two more dead! I gathered my men in front of our car for a head count. Of the 101 prisoners that had boarded with us there were only 62 survivors. You could now draw up the balance sheet of this trip: 39 dead since the start of Brno, about a 40% loss! If it was the same in the other cars something like 2,000 prisoners had died before arriving in the Donbass! Ruthless natural selection ......

The screams of our guards interrupted my thoughts. They shoot in the air to chase the Russian women away who came to us with buckets of water. They immediately fell back gesturing to the Russian soldiers in unmistakably crude signs of contempt. Surely these were mothers, and as everywhere they did not see us as enemies but just young men totally exhausted who could have been their own son or brothers. And they had to see one parade of prisoners after the other since the end of this war, or maybe even before. I was looking for Helmut in this chaotic crowd. Impossible!

I spoke to my men:

- Comrades, with the help of God we came out alive. We did not have water for so long but now the sky sent a refreshment. We will try to enter the camp with dignity, in rows of three, the weakest in the middle row to be supported from either side. The NCO with two soldiers make up the rear.

When the ranks were formed I counted the prisoners and made it clear to our guards that we were ready. It was not their problem, they said, their job had ended here. They returned to their rail car.

I went to the head of our little column, turning around in an attempt to give some courage to my soldiers. At the camp entrance an officer was supervising the columns of prisoners. Ours was the last to appear. Passing the officer, I gave him a military salute and he waved me to come to see him. My column stopped but he ordered them to continue. My leaving the head of my column had destabilized my men and he saw that I was concerned about their breaking ranks. Then in perfect German, he told me it would not matter. In the camp our well formed columns could dissolve and all the prisoners could mix. Then they would be directed to whatever barracks still had available space. For now they would be given food, a hot soup with bread. Then we would go through some health service and receive clean clothes. I should be at ease that I accepted his invitation to come to talk with him. I should no longer worry about having to take care of my comrades. But could I ever leave my responsibility for their well-being in his hands?

What they called 'barracks' were not much more than oversized huts crudely built from all kinds of left-over wood and corrugated steel. I followed him to an empty hut. Good opportunity to get rid of my watch. I pulled it from my pocket and I started to wind it after asking the commander for the present time. I offered it to him:

- You are the Commander of my men now. I no longer need my watch.

- Thank you, it's a great one, a German officer's watch. I'll give mine to my wife, she will be very happy.

His hut served as an office with three tables. We were still alone. The commander offered me water and I drink, again and again. I could have emptied a whole bucket! He looked at me in astonishment: "But didn't you have water during the trip?" His surprise seemed genuine. In times of peace, and even more in times of war it is a great asset if you quickly learn to judge people. I thought: this is a military man who can be trusted. So I told him about our trip in detail.

- I understand. It must have been a horror for you and your soldiers. I'll order a soup for you to have here.

Shortly, a plate with soup and brown bread was put in front of me. The officer let me devour my soup without really tasting it. It was such a blessing that I sent a look to the sky to thank God. The commander understood the meaning of my gesture. He asked me if I was a believer. I did not deny it. I even got the Virgin's medal and a cross out of the pouch that I wore around my neck telling him that I had received them from my mother the day I left for the war. He examined them carefully before returning them to me. Then I showed him my wallet which contained other memories of my mother, holy pictures, pictures of my cousins and friends that had died on the Russian front, each with a prayer card.

- Commander, I would like to keep those memories.

- I will take care of it.

After some hesitation, he continues:

- I'll let you move into a hut with other officers and few sick.

- Sick people ?

- Yes, and incurable. When the first convoys arrived here a week ago the prisoners came out of the cars and saw a small river nearby and they rushed to drink from it. Unfortunately, that water came directly from the mines and it is not drinkable. It triggers severe dysentery. We have nothing to treat them with. A German doctor advised me to give the prisoners charred bread as the only way to fight dysentery. But the poor guys were already completely dehydrated and they traded their bread against water with other prisoners. Result: those who swallowed the charred bread were cured and were placed under surveillance. For the other we had to dig new graves. We built additional latrines for those who can still move to get there. But often they lack the strength to return and they fall into the open latrine. It is horrible!

- Commander, thank you for putting me with other officers. But allow me to meet these patients as soon as possible. I want to talk to them. They need spiritual help.

He did not object but I could see in his eyes that my request was incomprehensible.

We left his office and he led me to another ranking officer in a white coat, the head of the health service. I understood that he gave instructions for safekeeping of my neck pouch and my wallet. I had to show them to the man in the white coat who made a note of them and then we continued our way to the officers' house. The commander took leave telling me to look for a place and, above all, not to say anything to anyone about our conversation.

*

In the officers' hut some form of a mattress seemed to wait for me. After the trials of my train ride this large potato sack filled with straw was superb comfort! My neighbor, a major, a big blond guy with blue eyes, immediately starts a conversation.

- Do I know the Russian officer who accompanied me?

- No, he just led me to this place for officers.

- Officers? Ha! It may be that there are some officers here, even a lieutenant colonel, the guy over there. A really bad guy! He even fought with a young soldier over a piece of bread!

- Maybe he is disguised as a lieutenant colonel to hide his true identity?
- Maybe. I'll deal with him before we go through the health service.
- Health service?
- Yes, I saw him at work, it is worth it!

We are getting ready for the 'health service'.

Upon leaving I see an officer with his white coat. He takes my pouch and my wallet. Then we pass other desks where they record our name, date of birth, father's name, and the last rank in the army. Next step: the showers. There is even a piece of soap. What a joy to wash ourselves!

And then, naked as were are, to be examined by nurses, such as they were. The one that examined me was the true image of a babushka with a merciless gaze. Armed with an old electric razor she starts cutting my hair, then she grabs my sex and quietly removes all my pubic hair. Then, using a razor with a dull blade she shaves my head and then gets rid of the last pubic hair, everywhere. To top off the session she spreads a white powder on all freshly shaved parts. The razor burn is painful beyond belief and I want to scream. The babushka fixes me a cold stare but I grit my teeth, determined not to let my pain show.

The final result depends on a female doctor examining us. Her exam was limited to one single gesture: pinching the buttocks of prisoners to judge their firmness to determine whether they would make good pack animals. I pass the exam successfully. She notes something in her records and "Dawai! Dawai!" Next! Last step, we are given old Red Army summer uniforms, shoes without laces with a cloth rag to wrap our feet and then an old empty quart size tin can. Our metamorphosis is accomplished. I am now a perfect prisoner of war.

The officer in the white coat hands me my wallet and my lucky charms. Nothing is missing. He gives me a piece of string pointing to my shoes, a good length of flexible wire to hold up my trousers and a spoon. He takes my tin can, punches a hole on each side and puts a piece of wire through them. I am now equipped fully for the duration of my life as prisoner. The next day I sharpened the handle of my spoon into a knife: perhaps one day there would be slices of a sausage or a piece of meat to be cut.

In addition to all this equipment, the man in the white coat had handed me a note from the commander inviting me to join him in the evening. I was hoping the officer would personally give my acceptance to the commander so that it does not fall into the wrong hands.

Back at the hut I find my neighbor. I look at him, he looks at me and we both burst out laughing. What a change! An hour ago we were still in our uniforms, with hair on our skull, and now in the uniform of the Red Army, shabby though clean. The major tells me the story of what happened to the Lieutenant Colonel in the health service. The guy who did the identity checking stumbled over some issues and took him away to some other hut. Since then, nobody has seen him. To me, this was most likely a Gestapo guy who wanted badly to go incognito.

Suddenly a young soldier calls me.

- Lieutenant! Do you remember me? I was with you in the car.

- Yes, I remember. Where are the others ?

- There are four or five in the hut next door with the sergeant and a corporal.

- Very good. I will see you later because I think the soup will be distributed soon. I also want to visit the sick. I will talk about it later.

- Be careful, said the major who had heard me. I do not want you to catch the virus. But after all, it's not my business. Anyway, no one talked to us about those patients.

I then told him the story of the polluted river, the dysentery, the dead and dying and how, after this episode, the commander had changed the point of arrival of prisoners to avoid the river.

*

46

A German prisoner was on duty at the sick bay keeping anyone from entering. About fifty men were dying in there. According to the guard they had no more than two days at the most. The mass grave was already dug and waiting. No one could do anything for them, even morally. So I had to go away thinking of the terrible loneliness of those poor guys who had to spend their last moments in this stench, suffering and abandoned. What would be going on in their minds? Even their names would fade into obscurity since they had not even had time to go through the registration process. It would be as if they had never existed. They would be 'unknown soldiers', referred to the nothingness of the 'missing'. May God grant them eternal peace at last! I was praying on my way to the hut of the commander, intrigued by his invitation.

He was waiting for me on the doorstep. We exchange military greetings but he immediately wants me to be aware of the codes of etiquette of the Red Army. Russian officers are addressed by "comrade", whether general or common soldier, all the same. Then the commander tells me about himself.

"Before 1930 and until the beginning of the rise of Hitler, at the request of the Soviet government, many German senior officers were sent to the Soviet Union to train senior officers of the Red Army. They used the German "Herr Major," "Herr General." For the new Soviet army it was excellent training. Besides, Germany also delivered weapons. Gone were the 'sloppy' communists. My father had often spoken to me of this Prussian discipline. Think of it: still today our army parades in goose step. Our first grand marshals of the old military tradition had created the first bodies of the Red Army on the Prussian system. But the majority of them were arrested in '36 or '37 and shot for 'high treason'. Stalin distrusted them all and above all he feared an army that would win the respect of the people. And so it continues. After the purges had deprived the Red Army of its best officers it was was reconstituted along the principles of the Communist Party. The new military elite owed everything to Stalin, it was entirely under his boot and under the control of political commissars. During the Patriotic War, the political commissars had unlimited power. We saw a little change starting in '44 when the new marshals of the Red Army have become indispensable. Now you know a little bit about our way of addressing each other. But now it is time to move to our dinner table."

- Commander, what about the officer who gave me your message and my answer to you?
- He is a man I can trust.

As I might have expected, the conversation was in part about my life in Germany before and during the war. He was impressed by my story, especially about the past six months.

Our dinner had ended and he answered a question that he saw was was burning on my lips:

- Where were you at the end of the war?

"I was still in East Prussia with the corps of Marshal Vasilevsky. Just between us, I have to tell you I was dazzled by the paved roads, the highways and especially by the beautiful houses, those that were still standing, and the large farms in the country side. We were not far from the Polish border in an area that had not been bombed. I had the opportunity to visit an abandoned two-story house. Everyone had fled seemingly at the last minute. The doors were not even locked. Everything was in place. It was beautiful: bathrooms with sinks, running hot and cold water. Same thing in the kitchen. I discovered there a much higher state of civilization than that of the Soviet Union! Suddenly, I understood how they had lied to us about everything. What a bunch of stories they made us swallow! I had changed my opinion about Germany. I understand that you are not a Nazi. When I finished my complete tour of that house I was wary, realizing that I could get into a lot of trouble if someone had found me out.

I looked around to make sure there was no one and I went quietly back to our tank regiment and my battalion. Everyone rested and some exhibited their war booty, watches, pans, spoons, knives, anything that was not too cumbersome to carry home. We were waiting for orders. My supervisor, a colonel who was only a year older than I knew no more. Finally, we, the officers, were given a few days of furlough just as the regiment was heading to Königsberg to assault the walled city. It was one of the bloodiest battles against the German army. Meanwhile we went on leave.

The train was packed with soldiers going home. They did not watch what they were saying about discovering the difference of life between Germany and the Soviet Union. I had noticed that some officers questioned others and laughingly emphasized the poverty of Soviet Russia and the modernity of Nazi Germany. One of them asked my opinion. I pretend I know nothing and that I had not had the opportunity to see anything. So he left me in peace.

When our train arrived in Moscow I saw that a lot of officers were taken away to a building while others, and I was one of them, were allowed to take their connecting trains. I went on to Donetsk where my family is. The war was winding down and I was made a reserve officer. I married a girl from Donetsk and at the end of May I moved here. I was appointed commander of the assembly camp for German prisoners of war which has existed since 1944. I have not told anyone about my German experience, neither my parents nor my wife. You are the only one to know. I know you never will speak of this conversation because you are aware of the danger facing me."

- Commander, I have not heard anything.

He shook both my hands before continuing:

"Tomorrow morning all able prisoners will leave for a nearby mining labor camp. The last patients will remain with a hundred men who will clean the barracks, build new latrines and do other work for about two weeks. As I will moved into a small shack with no comforts I would like, if possible, that you find some craftsmen to make it more habitable."

- Okay, show me your new hut tomorrow and I'll find the needed craftsmen.

- Good, let's go there and then we'll go 'home'.

In my hut everyone was asleep. I lay in silence, not without a last prayer to thank God for having made me meet a soldier who had given me his full confidence, just as He did with the SS captain in 1944. The affirmation of my faith had helped me open many doors. I had a good night.

*

Our neighbors in the other hut did not leave for the labor camp. I found my sergeant and four other survivors of our car and an officer called Bernard Hohmann. He came from the region of Erfurt. Luckily, he was a mason in civilian life and goes to recruit one or two carpenters and other workers.

- Very good. But do not tell any one about this story. I have an appointment at noon with the commander to show you his house. From what he said, there is a lot of work to be done.

At noon I share a soup with the commander and then we go see this house. It is small, very simple, newly built, standing there with nothing around. A young blonde woman appears in the doorway and the commander introduced me to his wife. I kiss her on the hand and everyone is pleasantly surprised. Inside, only the most basic furniture: two mattresses on the floor, a sink and mirror, two towels hanging from a nail and a bucket of water, a table, two chairs in a corner and a coat rack, all on a dirt floor. I suggest to the commander that I would return in the afternoon with the men to draw up plans and a time schedule.

Bernard had not been idle. He had assembled a good team and even found a young architecture student.

- Great, Bernard! I made an appointment with the commander for the afternoon to get organized. But most important is to find some building materials.

First, site meeting with brief presentations. Bernard asked the commander what he specifically wants done considering the coming autumn rains will make everything muddy and that winter will certainly be cold, so you have to think about installing a fireplace. The commander and his wife seem baffled. They do not know what to say. The notions of comfort and good life are not part of the Soviet priorities. I tell them no need to make decisions right now, let the specialists think about what can be done, then we can talk again. For now, we must address the issue of tools. We let Bernard and his team deal with that.

In the commander's office I ask for something to write with and a tape measure for my team. The commander is kind of shocked by this display of German efficiency. Most Russians do not have that mentality. Was it because they were living in poverty since the Bolshevik Revolution? To talk about something else, I note to the commander that there are very few guards in this huge camp.

- It has never happened here that a prisoner tried to escape. Currently, there are about a dozen guards for each hundred prisoners. The officer of health service will start tomorrow with cleaning the camp and all prisoners will be transferred elsewhere with new escorts.

He serves me a drink in an aluminum cup identical to his, while arguing about the differences of perceptions of life between Germans and Soviets. He wonders about the future of our two countries. What will be the answer? Fortunately, the arrival of Bernard and his team pulled me out of my embarrassment. They present their remodeling plans. The commander agrees to the interior and to improving the freeze protection of the well. However, any change in the outside appearance is out of the question. But why deny the development of the surroundings of the house? The architecture student has designed a nice garden, a fence, etc. The commander explains that we are in the Soviet Union and have our own lifestyle and it's best not to try to distinguish yourselves from anyone else.

- So let's stick to the plan to make the inside more livable and pleasant?
- Yes that's exactly it. What tools do you need? Just tell me and we will get them for you.

Passing the sick bay I see a prison commando cleaning and disinfecting. One hut is still under guard. Twenty men are dying in there.

*

I went to and from the camp. The project of the commander's house had lifted me out of my apathy.

- My word, Lieutenant, you now are like a true Russian! said a prisoner on duty outside one of the barracks where my workers had pilfered some planks as we were combing the camp for any buiding materials we could use.

It was true. The commander had given me a Russian army hat with the red star. It was not a luxury with the sun beating down hard!

- And where are the others?
- The health service officer came with an interpreter to form work teams. Right now, he shows them where to clean. We have ten days to finish.
- Very good. I'm with the commander in his hut.
- Yes sir. By the way, you remember me? I was in your car and since then I say my prayers every day.
- You're feeling better?
- Yes sir, and I found the will to live because I know God is with me.

I gave him an encouraging smile and he thanked me. Is it true that it does not take much to open the door that leads to God?

The commander and his wife were waiting for me. My team had suggested she leaves the house during construction. They told me that my men worked hard, they had received a full compliment of tools from the camp reserves and found two bags of cement. I wanted to see for myself about their work.

Indeed, the progress was obvious.

- Unless something extraordinary will happen everything will be completed in four days.

- No, Bernard, not in four days! Take two more before showing your work to the commander, otherwise we will have to work at camp cleaning. I will see you regularly and we will take stock.

On the third day Bernard tells me that they found enough materials to build a kitchen for Madame.

- Do your best. Are your meals taken care of?

- Yes sir, in the morning we eat at the camp. At noon and in the evening before we leave, they bring us our soup and bread, always the same guard. We get all the water we need right here. Furthermore, we improved the well water rigging.

- Congratulations! Let me know when you are done.

At each of my visits to the commander he compliments my men for their excellent work. Every night, he and his wife took a walk to the site, fully satisfied. And it was not a coincidence that it was the same guard who brought the food:

- Without a trusted man, I would never have undertaken this work. The guard is my wife's nephew but nobody knows. You understand the importance of keeping this to ourselves?

- Yes, sir.

On the sixth day in the afternoon, Bernard calls me. To my amazement the work was complete. Pulling themselves up by their shoestrings they had done the impossible. It just remains to clean up the place and put curtains on the two small windows. In an hour Bernard will bring two mattresses, a table and two chairs.

*

In their new house the commander and his wife were comfortably reading newspapers.

- Good news, sir?

- It's a Donetsk newspaper. The Americans will soon finish the Japanese. They continuously are bombarding Tokyo and other large cities.

- And the Red Army did not intervene to help the Americans in their advance?

- It is possible that the Americans did not ask.

Then he begins to talk about Stalin, the 'Little Father of the People' and his purges of intellectuals and scientists who are often Jews. He built concentration camps across the country for 're-education' through forced labor, as well as the deportation of millions. More than ten million Ukrainians had died of starvation in the 1930s. His grandfather told him about this terrible period. In the Donbass they were spared the purges thanks to our coal mines.

His wife did not understand a word of German. I had the impression that the commander had found a trusted partner to convey a message to the West in me:

"In the 30s, a certain 'Stakhanov' working in the coal mines of Donbass broke all the records of a day's coal production. He was honored in Moscow with the title of "Hero of the Soviet Union." From there on, Stalin ordered the implementation of production standards in all sectors, including in agriculture. You will soon get to know the system. But listen. My grandfather worked in the mines for forty years. Like everyone else, he has heard of the feat of Stakhanov. Except that no one has ever seen that man. The truth is that Stakhanov was a pure invention of Stalin. All this was before the war. Now that we've won the war, woe to the Russians who were taken prisoner by the German army between 1941 and 1942! They will be shipped to labor camps, subjected to ruthless living conditions so that they are crushed and can never aspire to the life they had discovered in the West. Stalin regards them as deserters. You may come across a few of them here and there."

- Do you have any news from the officers that went to Moscow?

- No, nothing. Anyway, it's dangerous to have relations between wartime comrades.

- Yes sir, now I understand the situation of the post-war Soviet Union a lot better.

Whereupon Bernard arrives with his team for the move carrying two additional chairs and a larger table. He asked us to wait a quarter of an hour. During this time the commander asks me to stress the importance to Bernard and his team not to speak about this work to other prisoners but to stick to the bare minimum of information, just enough to explain their absence.

What a surprise on entering the house! The wife of the commander is in heaven, so full of joy she kisses me on the mouth, followed in this by the commander! I was quite taken aback, but I had already noticed this custom at my time at the Kolkhoz! Bernard and his team are swamped with loud congratulations. The commander invites us to dinner.

Before starting the meal I invite the group to join me in a small prayer thanking the Lord for His daily bread. Amen. Surprise. The commander tells his wife and his nephew in Russian about the meaning of my prayer. They seem very moved.

We had an excellent dinner, the soup was very thick with white bread. Then back to our barracks.

Bernard told me on the way: "Lieutenant, you are an amazing man. Your faith in God seems unshakeable."

"My dear fellow, we know nothing of our future. Many of us will not survive but if you have faith in God he will help you keep up your courage and the will to live because you will know that God will never abandon you."

I then tell them about my mystical experience on Mount Scauri, at the beginning of the great offensive of Monte Cassino.

- And the Blessed Virgin Mary protect you, too. Try to stay together when we go to the new camp. Tomorrow morning I will see the commander to glean some information. Remember: do not talk to anyone, I mean no one, about your work with us in the commander's house. During the war we had the Gestapo on the back, you all know that. Here is the GPU. It's all the same. The life of a prisoners hangs by a thread and there is no other punishment than death. I think you heard me. Bernard, I count on you.

*

The next morning the commander said we would still spend another day here. Our departure is scheduled for the following morning after the soup to another camp 30 miles from here.

- The commander of this camp is a friend. I told him about you and your arrival there. You can trust him. He is a major like me, a reserve officer. In the beginnig you will work outside because the actual mine is flooded. Your registration dossier will accompany you everywhere until your release. I'll see you tomorrow morning at 9am.

- Does the new camp commander speak German like you?

- Yes, but do not say anything about it.

I thanked him warmly for his support and the most enjoyable time we had spent with him and his wife.

We left on a beautiful morning in mid-July of 1945. When we passed the commander I gave him my military salute, just as I had done when we had arrived.

*

CHAPTER 6

Making us Prisoners Indispensable

The new camp was 300 yards from the entrance to the mine. We had arrived around noon, slowed down by two controls. Hardly entered the new camp, another head count, new registrations and assignments of barracks. Phew! My 'team' did not leave my side. The major was also part of my group, along with some others from camp 1. The major's name is Friedrich, age 29, a native of East Prussia. His father was a general in the reserve and his parents own a castle with an imposing farmhouse on the Polish border. As the farm help were mostly Polish he speaks fluent Polish and understands Russian.

I limit my story to a minimum but Friedrich still is amazed that I am a lieutenant at at only 20 years with my Iron Cross 1st class and a medal for multiple injuries. His own journey is completely different. He was able to go to university before entering the military academy in Königsberg, appointed lieutenant at age 24. After the campaign in France he stayed in Paris until the end of '43, attached to the General Staff. Afterwards he got promoted to major and returned to the Königsberg military academy to teach which allowed him to spend all his weekends with his family. Realizing the advance of the Red Army his father had started to prepare his flight to Bavaria by buying a property there where he gradually transferred all his household. Now his father no longer had any personal relationship to the military academy and he did not know the new commander. This meant that he could no longer protect his son. Friedrich had received his marching orders for Italy in January '44 and joined the staff of our corps near Bologna. There he made himself a very good name. He remained in Italy until early September, which had not prevented him from traveling to Prague to visit with some of his close officer friends. In the Czechoslovak capital, he was attached to General Schörner's corps that at that time was still engaged in Silesia. At the end of the war he had lived in Prague.

Friedrich was perhaps expecting a story as detailed on my part but I remained cautious. He somehow struck me as a bit condescending with his aristocatic air. He obviously was accustomed to everybody treating him with much deference, especially the many Polish peasants who were toiling on his fathers huge estates. I gave him an abbreviated biography. Moreover, our conversation was interrupted by another prisoner entering the barrack in a Russian uniform:

- I'm your new delegate to the Commander. I come from Pomerania and I speak enough Russian. We apply the new camp rules. Each section will have an officer responsible to me. He alone will be able to contact the commander to defend the rights of prisoners. How many officers are in here? (We were three.) Who proposes to be the responsible one?

I raise my arm. The delegate noted my name and rank. Major Friedrich and another officer left our hut with the delegate. Actually, I was pretty happy that Friedrich had left. His presence made me ill at ease, I did not feel he was a good comrade, instead he had some kind of aura of danger about him.

By early afternoon, all the responsible officers were called to the camp commander. Knowing we were thirty-two officers and every section had fifty prisoners, this meant that there were 1600 prisoners in the camp. The delegate presented each officer to the commander and then outlined the schedule: up at 7am for soup and a serving of bread for the day, starting for the mine at 8am. Officials of the mine would organize the work programs. At 6pm back to the camp on foot.

At dismissal the delegate takes me aside. The commander wants to talk to me. Left alone with him, he askes me point blank if I am a believer.

- Yes sir, and I would like to keep my private things.
- Do you have them on you?

I showed them to him. He agreed to let me have them.

- I'll note it in your file because here I could be replaced any time.

On the way back I was thinking that life for labor camp commanders was quite different from the one they had in the army. Those I had met since my capture seemed extremely cautious, close to paranoia. Probably they fear the men of the GPU that had infiltrated everywhere.

When I arrived in the central square, I came across Bernard and the young architect. They stand in front of an empty billboard.

- Lieutenant, I think we should post the news about our new camp here.
- Maybe, but first tell me where are the latrines?
- Follow me.

A strong smell of chlorine emanated from the place.

- Inside there is a chlorine bag with a small shovel.
- And everyone has to sprinkle his shit?
- Yes sir, an old prisoner has explained everything. And it is the same in all the camps.
- At least this one is closed and there is a roof!

The next morning, first day of work. The Director of the Mine complex quickly directed us to different work sites and mines. These mines were nothing like the ones we remembered from Germany and France. There was only minimal equipment. Some of the 'mines' were little more than narrow tunnels carved into the hillside.

With my fifty men we are assigned to the first mine to prepare the support beams galleries. The tools could not have been more archaic and yet we would have to make the best of it. Future miners' lives, including our own, would depend on the strength of these beams. It made things easier that most of the Russian mining officials spoke some German. Soon enough one of their mining engineers explained their predicament: "The Red Army had dismantled most of the equipment of the mines in Silesia and sent it to us, among others the motors for our water pumps and for the elevators, but our systems fail almost every day. As a result our mine is always flooded, just as almost every other of our mines here."

- Do you have mechanics here to fix this?

- Yes, but they do not know how.

- If it's like that, let me try to find some specialists.

- Could you really? That would be great because then we might be able to fill our work 'norms' and we would get our full pay!!

-Ah !

-Yes, the famous Stakhanov standards. We heard about that.

I saw a perfect opportunity to take the lead and to make ourselves indispensable.

I asked my fellow prisoners:

- Do we have in our group any mechanics, electricians or even engineers? The mines management needs our help.

As the Russian remained at my side, I could not go into details. Bernard came to me to ask what all that meant. I took him aside and explained quickly that I saw an opportunity to better our situation by showing these Russians what good German craftsmanship is able to do. He promised to take care of everything.

I took the Russian engineer by the arm and walked away with him to talk a little about our plan.

- We'll take care of your problem. What is your function here?

- We are seven officials, the director, his deputy, myself and four others. Come, I'll introduce you to the director.

The director agreed with my proposal to help. He spoke pretty decent German:

- Soon the soup at noon, after that you organize everything. I trust you, you Germans are good specialists.

I got together with my team. Bernard introduced me to two engineers, four mechanics and several other craftsmen.

- Comrades, we have a chance to make ourselves indispensable and enjoy various benefits. If you are able get their mines going and if you follow my orders, we will be masters of this site in a short time, but be careful and maintain discipline!

My team went to work. Two hours later the deputy came running to me: the motors were running again! He ran to inform his superior.

*

After the soup Bernard and I walked while discussing our new activity at the mine:

- Bernard, never forget that your relationship with the deputy director shall be limited strictly to labor issues and nothing else. If he asks you anything else, tell him to contact me.

- Yes, sir. I understand.

I remembered the French prisoners in Germany at the beginning of the war when I was still at my parents and the trouble they caused my father because of their carelessness with their packages from home. That's why I was determined to give structure and purpose to these defenseless men, to help them overcome the demoralizing status as prisoners, to give them someone who would look after them and enforces discipline. Discipline must be the norm, since it offers some measure of protection.

The next day we start again for the mine. Congratulations from the director. Both motors are still working and pump water in a steady stream like a small river. A good chance that the mine could become operational again soon.

- But this water is not drinkable, it is toxic.

- Of course ! You must not drink it and everybody knows it. And further down the water gets lost in the river.

Really? Meanwhile, 5000 of our men had died because of this rotten river. No comment! Shaking off my anger I ask:

- What is our program today?

- I think your three specialists should remain near the engines to monitor their operation. I did deliver gasoline and oil.

- And your own mechanics?

- I sent them back.

- And the other men in my team?

- They should continue to make support beams, because we need a large amount.

- And me ?

- You work with me.

He led me into his office:

"In a few days we will receive the plans for a major facility capable of running at least ten mines. This is a very good program and I count on you to provide me with a competent staff."

- I will do my best, but I guess these new projects require engineers.

- Do you have you have some ?

- Yes, according to the director we have some excellent engineers.

- Then it's perfect.

He took me by the arm and whispered whether he could always count on me. Apparently he did not have much faith in his engineers' abilities.

In the evening we were told to drop everything and to assemble at the central square. Our prisoner delegate had learned that there would be a newspaper for us prisoners pinned to the billboard. I could not wait to compare Soviet propaganda to that of the Nazis. Probably difficult to tell apart! A real festival of tall tales full of the same arrogance! We learned, however, that the American war against Japan was not yet over.

There were about thirty men huddled together in front of the billboard and not everyone could get close enough to read, therefore, they asked me to read it for them:

"Headline: Japan has not surrendered and the Pacific war continues. American bombers destroyed the Japanese cities one after the other since the Japanese government rejected an ultimatum from the US high command late in July. Reconstruction of the Soviet homeland made great progress thanks to the heroes of the war coming to help our population in this heavy task." I turned to my friends asking who knew about the Pacific War. No one! Early 1942, I had heard on the radio that Japan, an ally of the Axis Germany-Italy, had destroyed US navy forces in Hawaii and declared war on the Americans. Then I was drafted for the Works Service and I left for Russia. After that, silence, no news of the US-Japanese battles!

Maybe I could learn more from my Russian masters? I asked the mines manager. He did not know much either. He nevertheless promised to check with the director of the mining complex because he read the regional newspaper. And through newspapers lent by the 'big boss', the director could give me a short press review. Actually, I knew most of the news. What interested me was the Japan-US war. He said "da-da" and added that the director wanted to meet me. I was on my guard:

- Why does he want to see me?

- You know I need the support of the director of the complex, he is very powerful and I depend entirely on him. Since you have given me good advice I spoke to him about you.

- By the way, what's your name?

- Alexander.

- Great! Alexander the Great!

What had I said! Any reference to such a historic figure was totally banned in the Soviet Union. I reassure him, I'll never make reference to Alexander the Great again. The terror was everywhere on this earth but the Stalinist terror was the worst.

The next day with Alexander, I met the director. He questions me. Am I interested in politics?

- Politics ? Not at all. Simply, at the end of '41, when I was still at my parents, I heard on the radio that Japan had attacked the Americans and destroyed their entire Pacific Fleet in Hawaii. After that they declared war on the Americans. And I read in the prisoners' newspaper that the war between Japan and the United States was not yet finished, I was surprised, because we are already were in mid-August of '45.

- Wait for tomorrow and you will have more news on display. Let me tell you that I appreciate the help you have given to the mine manager. Why have you done that?

- The German army has done much harm to your country and especially to your mining industry. I see our role as prisoners of war to help you to bring your mines back into production because your country needs coal very badly. We are all men, we need each other. And with God's help, we will eventually better understand and appreciate each other.

He shook my hand and gave me an appointment the next day to talk about organization.

In the morning Alexander led me directly to his superior.

- What's his name?

- His name is difficult to pronounce but not his first name: Karel. We'll see how he will react.

He was already waiting for us:

- My name is Karel. It's easier. I know your name already. Come, tell me how you can help us.

- In each group of prisoners we have mechanics who can service your water pumps. Others are carpenters or lumberjacks who can manufacture support beams. Some of us are engineers, not to mention masons who could build foundations for the mine elevators. But I think you also have excellent engineers to direct most of the work. For the beams your hardware is not up to date.

Maybe you can find better tools that would increase production. If we work together we could meet and even exceed your work norms!

The director exchanged a knowing glance with Alexander and nodded. I had touched a sensitive point: their infamous work 'norms'! But I wanted to know more about Karel:

- You speak impeccable German. Where did you learn it?
- In Berlin. By the time I finished my university studies the Russian and German governments had agreed to organize student exchanges so that young Russians could perfect their German in Berlin and young Germans their Russian in Moscow. This was organized through the embassies. I stayed one year in Berlin lodged near the embassy.

In the evening a new copy of the newspaper was displayed. As before, I began to read aloud:

"Japan surrendered unconditionally and stopped all hostility on August 15, 1945. On August 6 the US imperialist-capitalist dropped an atomic bomb on Hiroshima and completely destroyed the city killing most of its people. On August 8 Marshal Stalin declared war on Japan and launched the Red Army against the Japanese in Manchuria and liberated the Kuril Islands in the north of Japan. On August 9, the Americans dropped a second atomic bomb on Nagasaki destroying the city and its people. Thanks to the intervention of the Red Army the Americans won the war against Japan!"

I was careful not to make any comment on the conclusion of the article.

I continued to talk but I did not read:
- Japan was destroyed by US forces. When the Japanese attacked Hawaii they did not know they were awakening a giant that would put them to their knees, but they also will help them become a democracy.

Soon many prisoners had joined to listen to my reading of the newspaper. Moved by the feeling of living a historic moment, I spoke:

- My dear comrades, the Second World War is really over. A new era begins!

No reaction. Nothing. My words were lost to the silent dejection and apathy of the 200 men before me. I then asked if, apart from the Germans, there were other Europeans among us. Arms were raised up: Austrians, French, Italians, Hungarians, Belgians. So I shouted:

- Since we are all Europeans, I officially declare the birth of the United States of Europe!

After a few moments of of stupor, frantic applause broke out and I continued, tears in my eyes:

- Comrades, Europe is in ruins and ashes. It's time to rebuild our nations into one great country, let's shout "long live the United States of Europe!" If God helps us find our families, let us be the first builders and defenders of our new homeland: the United States of Europe!

I had the impression of being struck by a dream and to share in making it a reality. The prospect of a European president, a government, a common foreign policy and an army to defend our freedom had warmed the heart of the prisoners. For a moment we all forgot our uncertain future. Somehow I had given them hope for a better world. I was happy to have awakened in my friends a new courage to move forward.

After this 'historic' moment it was necessary to get back down to earth. I counted 'my' little band. Fifty prisoners were present in neat rows of four. Bernard, another sergeant and I always wanted to present ourselves in order for the evening meal. I gave a military salute with the words "Section 3, present for the soup." It was meant to impress the soup chef and somehow we got ample portions and a thick slice of bread.

After our 'dinner' Bernard said to me:

- Lieutenant, come with me, you have not read everything in the newspaper.

It was true. I jumped at the news of Europe and especially those of Germany. According to this paper, the occupied area of

Eastern Germany was being rebuilt with the help of the Soviet Union, while the West Zone, occupied by US and British forces, lacked everything. No food or water, and the first signs of an an epidemic is announced. It was also announced, in small print, that the Americans had discovered the concentration camps in Germany with thousands of dead people! Then came an endless stream of Soviet propaganda on the theme of Russia's renewal thanks to the mobilization of all the liberated people.

Back in my barrack I met our prisoner delegate.

- I heard about your proclamation of a 'United States of Europe' and the enthusiasm of the prisoners. It was great to cheer up all those poor people.

- Poor people, why?

- In '44, when the Red Army arrived in Poland I deserted my fighting unit and I was made prisoner. I have been incorporated into the Red Army and I trained as a propagandist. Under the orders of a political commissar we spent the night making speeches over loud speakers to tell German soldiers to desert and join us with promises that were never kept. Those who had taken the bait were immediately dispatched to labor camps and many died before the end of the war. But the worst I have seen with my own eyes was the behavior of Russian soldiers. Arriving in villages and small towns of Poland they raped women of all ages, even children as young as 10! Poland is a very Catholic country and their priests wanted to help these unfortunate. Then the soldiers stuffed them with vodka and propaganda and beat them, and some were crucified on doors. It was horrible, I never talked about it. But if you return one day to Germany I would like you to talk to them about the crimes of the Red Army.

- I too have seen with my own eyes that kind of horrors, but it was in Germany. I did not know that Poland had suffered the same savagery!

- Never tell anyone here about this because the GPU has ears everywhere.

- Don't worry.

- I trust you. By the way, the commander wants to see you.

- Why ?

- I do not know.

The commander's office was very simple, a table, two chairs and a telephone. He came right to the heart of the matter: my contacts with the mine officials and my initiatives to organize help. I shut up.

- The director of the mine called me and asked me if you could find other specialists for other mines.

- Commander, I suggest you to organize a meeting with all responsible officers to tell them about this request of the director of the complex, but without mentioning my name.

- Okay, I'll do it immediately. Something else. You read the prisoner newspaper?

- Yes sir.

- You saw that World War II ended on August 15?

- Yes sir.

- And you mentioned your desire to create the 'United States of Europe'?

- Yes sir, because that is the only way to prevent our people from getting into a new war.

He looked at me and away from the phone, whispered:

- This was a political declaration and politics are strictly forbidden for all prisoners of war. But you are a believer and your good intentions gave your men new courage.

Then he reiterated his thanks for the help that we had given to mine managers. He took my hands, putting a finger to his lips. Yes, the walls have ears.

Upon leaving I came face to face with two aged prisoners. One of them opens up to me:

- We heard you read the newspaper which as usual we never read. This gave us courage. We were at Stalingrad and our company was captured on Christmas 1942. We were in the far north of the city when the Russians surprised us. Our company commander gave us the order to surrender. We are perhaps the first prisoners of Stalingrad and we'd like be in your barracks, if possible.

- Where are you currently ?

- Right next to yours, and eight of our age are in another camp.

- I'll arrange it tomorrow. Have courage and believe in God. He will not abandon you.

*

CHAPTER 7

Trying to put Order into our Prison Lives

In the evening the two former Stalingrad men were waiting for me in front of our hut. Two young soldiers had ceded their places without fuss. The officer in charge did not mind. I introduced the two veterans to my comrades and we lined up to go to get the soup.

The evenings in the Donbass at the end of August were sweet. We religiously savored those moments of peace. Then we went back into our hut and I asked the two survivors of Stalingrad to tell us about their lives as prisoners until today.

One of these men was 30, NCO, the other 32, a Chief Warrant Officer. Both began by thanking me for having accepted them in our group because since my statement of "United States of Europe" last night they held me in high esteem:

- Since our capture by the Russians at Christmas '42 we have never found such a good atmosphere. This here is a little like heaven on earth. Lieutenant, maybe it's because you have maintained some discipline?

Bernard beat me to it:

- When you told us your age, I was very surprised because I would have given you almost 50 years. You had to suffer terribly. Ever since we were with Lieutenant Pappert we feel safe. He did everything he could for us. His words are always thoughtful. Thanks to him, some of us have found faith in God.

- Bernard, I am pleased to hear you say that but I want our two comrades tell us a little of their lives since Christmas 1942.

The Chief Warrant Officer took the floor:

"Before Christmas we learned that the Red Army had managed to encircle Stalingrad from the west and now we no longer could count on reinforcement troops to come to give us a hand. Anyway, there were no more reserve troops. Occasionally, a plane managed to drop food, provided the parachutes came down near our lines. Until early December the Junkers 52 airplanes could land near us and supply us with food, medicine and letters. They took the seriously wounded, our mail and urgent requests for support. Their landings became more and more rare as low clouds, fog and snow prevented landing. Towards Christmas everything stopped for good. On Christmas Day, we had a small tree in a large cellar which was our rest area. The battle raged in the center, but for us, to the north, it was rather quiet. The night had fallen, we were given a meal, a little better than usual, with a bottle of beer. At the end of the meal, we started singing Christmas carols and suddenly the cellar door was shattered, ten Russians emerged screaming: "Hands up!" Our lieutenant ordered us not to resist, it was useless. They disarmed us and took us out into the cold night where we found our own guard detail which had been arrested also together with my friend here who had been in charge. We bypassed the last German defenses and one mile further, we were put in the middle of a very large entrenchment of Russian troops and weapons. We were directed to a large building and we had to take off our uniforms. We were given old Soviet army pants, jackets and coats, many torn, often without buttons, and felt boots and then pointed hats with the Red Star. From there we went to our first camp.

This camp was at a rail station. Our job was to unload the trains and load trucks that left immediately to the front. The food we got was a bare minimum. After three weeks on this diet, we were pushed into other trucks that took us further north. We rode all day on snowy roads before arriving in another prison camp. There were already between 1000 or 2000 German soldiers and officers. This is where our nightmare really began. Every day we had to clear the snow from the roads and remove the ice. We worked without gloves and our hands almost froze. We rubbed them between our legs to try to warm them up a bit. In the evening we were given hot soup and one slice of bread. Our barracks were not heated and there was no light. We had been given some worn blankets but not enough for everyone. So we would lay close to each other to keep warm. It was hell in the morning to get up and unfold. We waited anxiously for our soup, not a very thick soup but at least it was something warm. And then 'Dawai! Dawai', back to work in the snow, with a good rifle butt in the kidneys for encouragement.

There were those who let themselves die of hunger and the piercing cold. As the earth was frozen they left the bodies in the open and completely naked as we took all their clothing so that we had a little more to wear. I never saw or heard anyone pray during my military service or at the front. During the war we received orders, we obeyed, and that was it."

- Yes, it was exactly like that, the NCO said.

"When spring finally arrived, those who had survived the winter were taken to another camp of about 10,000 prisoners, the largest in the back country, near a kolkhoz. The guards were either very old or very young, not old military men as here. They were full of hatred, no mercy for us 'invaders'. We worked in the fields under the orders of the kolkhoz personnel. The same kolkhoz people supplied our meals, always the same menu: potato soup and some black bread. At least it was much better than what we got in our previous camp and we regained some strength and morale improved somewhat. In autumn '43, after the harvest, we were sent to different camps in the south to reconstruct railways in the Donetsk area. We arrived in the Donbass in the beginning of the year, always continuing track repair. Some that were captured as late as '44 joined us there. At that time there were not many of us former Stalingrad men left. We got lucky for having landed here. A true haven of peace compared with......"

They had tears in their eyes.

- Yes, for the moment. So far we had former military officers with whom to negotiate and we could convince them that decent living conditions would be good not only for us but also for them.

No sooner had I said those words the prisoner delegate appeared, asking me to follow him to the commander.

Why would the commander want to see me at such a late hour? The delegate did not know. It turned out that there had been no special urgency for this meeting. At first the commander thanked me for my initiative to provide qualified personnel to the mines management:

- In this regard, the director of the complex called to tell me that all the officers have accepted the new rules and there is excellent cooperation between the directors of mines and the officers responsible for their groups of prisoners. Karel asked me to inform you that he has done everything to get better tools for the manufacture of the beams. Just for your information, the camp commanders and the directors of the mining complex are all superior officers, but the mine managers are just lieutenants.

- Thank you for making that clear to us.

I was about to leave.

- One moment please. The director of a kolkhoz just asked for some men to help with the melons harvest. If you are interested in working outdoors for a day you can do that.

- With pleasure, sir.

- We need about 300 men. Do you have a preference ?

- No sir, I leave the choice to you. I am happy to announce this news to my men.

The next morning at the mine I went to see Karel in his office:

- You really have very good people among you. You certainly know that your commander is a Lieutenant Colonel? And you ?

- Me, I'm a Major and Alexander is a Lieutenant like you. This remains between us but, you know, the intervention by the Red Army has not caused the Japanese surrender. It is the Japanese emperor who has prevailed on his government. He understood that the power of the Americans would put his country to its knees and cause the loss of many Japanese in an already devastated country, reducing everyone to abject poverty. Alexander and I are of the same opinion. Stalin did too much harm to our families. We are Ukrainians and many of our family members died of starvation or deportation as a result of Stalin's agricultural policies.

With that, we congratulate each other like three conspirators!

That evening I told my men that the next day we would go to the countryside to harvest melons, a gift from the commander. The evening was spent in a good and relaxed atmosphere.

*

Tightly squeezed into trucks we 300 men were on our way to the kolkhoz, some twenty miles away. We had just one guard per truck, knowing that the kolkhoz staff would take care of us.

They quickly explained to us that it was the last day of harvest, and a lot of melons were already rotten. We should pick the healthy fruits and each of us would receive one later in the day.

We worked by fours, the first detached melons with an ax, the other three were collecting them, filled bins which they loaded on trucks parked everywhere. For the first time in my life I saw a melon. Even in 1942 with the Work Service in Russia, near Kursk, I had not seen any. At noon we returned to the kolkhoz for melon soup with bread. Unusual for us but not bad.

Returning to the collection I spotted a new guard, youngish, giving signs of nervousness. We changed to another field. Russian women were harvesting sunflowers. While working they crunched sunflower seeds between their teeth. The took the seeds into one side of their mouths and spit out the empty shells from the other side, all at an incredible speed! At the same time they sang quite melancholic melodies, while the men supervising their work kept yelling their infernal "Dawai! Dawai!"

Our young soldier-guard also began yelling at us melon pickers and approached with a menacing look on his face. Suddenly, he raised his gun and shoots over the head of a young prisoner. Unleashing a barrage of yelling, hitting the prisoner with his rifle butt, kicking him with his boots, with 'I will kill you'. Something had to be done. I ask my men to shout with all their might to alert someone. A big guy shows up, fires into the air, shouts orders at this guard, disarms him and chases him away. I will never forget the intervention of this soldier, probably an officer. He was tall, blond, blue eyes, his belt cinched at the waist, showing his broad shoulders. A perfect athlete.

Our poor prisoner was a mess, semi-conscious, his face beaten to a pulp, probably with some broken teeth. Two men arrived and took him with them without comment, but where?

In the evening, as promised, each of us has had the right to a melon or watermelon. I chose a melon for me and one for the beaten young soldier. The kolkhoz guy did not understand why I wanted a second melon. He called a colleague who spoke some German. I explained that this second melon was for the young prisoner seriously wounded by the guard.

At the camp I immediately reported the sad incident to the commander and asked where the young prisoner was. The guards were not his responsibility, all he could do was to try to find out about it.

Later, the prisoner delegate said that the young soldier had been transported to the camp hospital. Impossible to know more.

- Between us I can tell you that this man will never heal. I know how it goes.

- I see. Another question: have you ever participated in the harvest of melons?

- No never.

- Well, I give you the melon that was intended for the young soldier who will never heal.

The delegate had never tasted a melon before.

*

Very few Russian guards were watching us at the mine. While my men got set to work Alexander motioned to me:

- The mine's installation drawings have arrived and we can start with the construction of the engine foundations. Karel wants to see you as soon as possible.

- Let's go.

Four other people were in Karel's office:

-These are the four chief engineers responsible for the construction and functioning of the new equipment. We expect equipment for ten of the mines. Each mine will have three engineers to direct the work under the supervision of four senior engineers. I count on your cooperation as before.

The engineers started their work.

- We're now in early September. We have no more than one month to build the foundations and to install the motors. In October we risk the first frost. We must therefore complete the installation as soon as possible. Will all the materials for all ten mines arrive together?

- No, we receive one complete set of equipment in two or three days and the rest about a week later.

- I know a building engineer. I propose to get him into my team.

- If you want, it's okay.

Alexander and I left Karel's office and we continued to discuss the work organization:

- Alexander, can we do the first of the installations here in your mine?
- Yes, that is what is expected.
- So my engineer can do his work without interference. If he has a point to make he will address it to you.
- Ah yes, while Karel is a very intelligent man he is no more an engineer than I am! But if we have problems with finishing our work and the elevators do not work at the end of September we will be in big trouble!
- Trust me, Alexander, I'll find a solution.

In truth, I was not sure of anything, except that Alexander was visibly very concerned.

We had lunch together. He invited his deputy and we chatted about everything and nothing, Alexander spoke of future work, his deputy was delighted that his mine was chosen to be first. I did not go into details, aware that Alexander did not want to share his fears with his deputy.

He suddenly came up with a proposal:
- Comrade director, one of our assistants would like to give a demonstration in the presence of the Lieutenant.
- Why in his presence?
- I do not know but he said it would be a surprise for everyone.

The assistant in question was waiting outside Alexander's office, a shack standing on a slab of soil and cement while the upper part, equipped with windows, was wood. The man was in his thirties. He was holding a hammer and a mason's metal edge. He asked Alexander permission to drill a small hole in the wall, after which he takes from his pocket an object wrapped in a cloth and unpack it with the precautions of a jeweler with a rare piece. It was a nickel faucet. He rubs it vigorously and then screws it into the hole. Then, with a triumphant smile, he turns handle of the valve as if to open it, then closes it, opens it again, turns it in all directions and does not understand what is happening, that is to say, of course, nothing. He is astonished, and as he dismantled the faucet he mumbles that in Germany the water would flow smoothly....

The scene is both funny and pathetic. Alexander gives the man some explanation. The poor guy opened his eyes wide like saucers. Alexander turns with a sigh.

- Many of our soldiers were intrigued with many aspects of progress in your country and returned with a whole bunch of objects they had removed from homes there. In their unbelievable ignorance they imagined that all these gadgets would work the same when they installed them in their homes and they all are surprised when it does not work. Even in Donetsk we do not have running water.

I stayed with Alexander and we resumed our conversation on the follow up of the work as it would progress. One always had to reassure him. At the rate Bernard and his two mechanics worked our mine would be pumped dry before the end of September. To make sure Bernard went to recruit additional help that evening.

I had learned from the commander that there were twelve mining complexes in the region, that means twelve labor camps. Conclusion: we must have between 25 and 30 000 prisoners in the Donbass.

Still enjoying the pleasant temperature we ate our soup to cool off before returning. Bernard explained to our group our next job in the mine and asked who had good construction experience. Several hands went up. Bernard noted that we had a building engineer, Wilhelm, several bricklayers and one concrete specialist.

- Excellent! Tomorrow I present our work plans to the Director of our mine.

*

We had a good night, my men were in good shape. I made them form our usual three men deep column and we marched past the commander as if we were on parade, greeting him with our military salute to which he responded with a wry smile. A bit down the road I stopped my men to express my gratitude and appreciation for their willingness to show what we German prisoners would be able to do: "I'm proud of you!" You could read in their eyes the joy and happiness of being a well-knit group with a new found purpose in their drab lives, and also to have found someone who understands them and offers them protection, all the things that are so painfully absent in prison camps.

I presented our building engineer Wilhelm to Alexander who was on the telephone with Karel. I took the opportunity to find out more about Wilhelm: he is 32, from Hamburg, studied civil engineering, drafted into military service in Hamburg, sent to the front in 1944, first to Italy and then to Czechoslovakia where he was taken prisoner.

With him our team was complete and we were able to take stock. Wilhelm surprised us by the depth of his knowledge. He was the man for the situation. He saw nothing insurmountable but he suggested a "technical coordination meeting" with the head of the Russian engineers.

- Good. This afternoon, you will come with Alexander to meet with their engineer in charge. He speaks excellent German and knows the technical vocabulary in your language. Like me he is Ukrainian but the others are Russian.

These Russian engineers made Alexander uneasy and he did not hide his concerns.

- Alexander, don't worry. Our engineers are very competent but they also have a good sense of hierarchy and know how to behave in front of a Russian in charge. You already had proof that we know our work while respecting your authority.

He raised his arms inagreement, as someone who thinks, "Let's hope it lasts!" While he was telephoning, I said to Wilhelm:

- I think you understand the problem. Karel is responsible for this complex and he is not an engineer. Ditto for Alexander. They are dependent on the decisions of their Russian engineers and they fear them. They are not the only ones.

- Lieutenant, don't worry, We understand the situation. This afternoon everything will be fine.

The Russian chief engineer was a very big man. Wilhelm arises to the occasion and it seems that there is immediately a good rapport between the two men. They are already deep in a professional exchange. We see that they understand each other. Soon the engineer thanks Wilhelm, commenting in passing about the difference in training between Russians and Germans, much to the advantage of the latter:

- I think we'll work well together. As for my fellow engineers, I will undertake to convince them to cooperate because they are much afraid that we can not get done on time.

After the chief had left Karel thanked us warmly:

- You have a strong sense of organization and you are surrounded by professionals that are not easily found here. Besides, I have not forgotten what you told me that you were aware that as POWs you have some kind of moral obligation to help in repairing the destruction caused by your army. We cannot achieve this without each other, and with God's help, we will get there. You are a believer and being a believer is a guarantee of trust.

Wilhelm looked at me as if he were discovering me.

Alexander invited us to have a cup of tea:

- You know, we the directors of mines and complex managers, we are entitled to afternoon tea with white bread and fruit flavored sugar. Come and have tea with me.

We had a great afternoon chatting along very much at ease, especially about what makes the difference between the training of young Germans and their Soviet counterparts. Alexander asked Wilhelm if we had other engineers in our camp. He was surprised to learn that among the 1600 prisoners just about all trades were represented.

- You know, Alexander, I continued, there was a very well stablished system of technical training well before Hitler. Young people who could not continue their studies for various reasons, learned a craft, like bricklayer, carpenter, butcher, whatever. The others went to college to become engineers, scientists, politicians. In any case, we had to undergo very specialized examinations before we could apply for jobs.

- Yes, we can say that we have lived and are living in two very different worlds, said Alexander.

I thanked him for this relaxed mutual exchange. We shook hands very friendly.

*

It became a habit: the camp commander always wanted to meet with me as soon as we were back, as if he expected me to give him a daily report. Most of the time he initiated the conversation with praise for my role as coordinator, all thanks to Karel.

- I am particularly pleased that you as a believer have managed so quickly to bridge the gap between winners and losers. This is a very good example of brotherhood among men from different worlds. After supper I'd like to see you again.

- Aye sir.

I wanted to give him a military salute but he shook my hand.

Evenings so late in the season were still very pleasant in the Donbass. Was it the proximity to the Black Sea? The moments that followed the meal led to quiet walks in the camp. Once again I had an appointment with the commander. In his office, the phone was disconnected. He saw that this detail had not escaped me:

"As you can imagine here all officials are under constant surveillance, including Karel. You will recall that the camp commanders never stay long in one place. It's part of the Soviet system. Our senior managers all belong to the GPU, they are political commissars. They distrust us for the simple reason that the camp commanders are former military officers. They fear that we might fraternize with prisoners who are also military and we let ourselves be impressed by their expertise. But rest assured, the GPU is aware of the good work you do in the mines. I just wanted to warn you that I may be soon transferred to another camp. This always happens at night. In other words, if one morning you discover a new commander do not be surprised. If the new commander is accompanied by an officer wearing red epaulettes and a red band on his cap you should know that this is a political commissar. In this case, my successor will have no power, he will just execute the orders of the Commissar. Then I advise you not to leave the camp in rows and with discipline but rather shuffled and messy. Ditto when you go to get your soup. You should not let these political commissars know that you have kept your dignity and your sense of the military hierarchy.

They prefer to see the prisoners subdued and more like a band of misfits, it reassures them. But at the mine you will continue to report to the managers, in your case Karel. Another thing: the beginning of October, as a precaution, I will install coal stoves in the barracks in anticipation of winter. One last tip. The work of political commissars is to break the will of prisoners. Never rebel, but keep your faith. This gives you a great inner strength. I am a soldier from my youth, I commanded an infantry regiment, and it was not until early 1944 after an injury I had to take on a labor camp, in the Donbass, more to the north where I encountered the first German prisoners. Many were survivors of Stalingrad, unable to do real work, they were too emaciated and weak. Even when I could get them better food they let themselves die. Nobody was there to give them hope."

- Commander, I met a Russian Orthodox priest among some of your combatants. A young officer told me that they were scattered everywhere, hidden in the uniform of a common soldier. If they were to be discovered by a political commissar it would mean twelve bullets.

I told him of our battle at Hirschberg on Mount Coffin. The commander simply concluded that religion made brave men. Finally, he wished me good luck in spending the winter here because -30F ° was not uncommon.

The next day the commander was no longer here.

At the mine I found Wilhelm, the engineer, in the best frame of mind.

The rest of the new mining equipment had arrived and four days later the elevators ran perfectly. Of course, we still could not go down into the mine, too much of it still flooded, but the successful start-up of the first elevator set an optimistic tone for the entire complex. The Russian engineers were happy to watch the Germans at work. Karel was delighted. If the pumps would hold out, actual mining could start still in September. Support beam production had doubled since we had been given better tools. Everything seemed fine.

The new commander had arrived at the camp. He is young and barely looked at us. I told my comrades:

- We have a new commander. This means the rules will be changed. Caution. Try not to be noticed. No more walking in rank and do not show any signs of discipline among you and your fellow prisoners. We do not know yet how the new commander will act. We will advise you later.

The following days our teams continued to work well beating all the targets. Karel was full of praise. The arrival of a new commander did not surprise him.

- You will see that the new guy will be 'ok' because he will realize that I need competent men to get production started.

- I hope, Karel.

- But yes! I know the system. Everyone distrusts his neighbor, except prisoners of war. No mistrust vis-à-vis them.

Let's hope so.

*

CHAPTER 8

The Good, the Bad, and the Joy of Faith

On September 25, 1945, we returned quietly to camp after a good days work with the feeling of accomplishment. But what a welcome!

An officer that we did not know screams in Russian and shakes like a man possessed, flanked by the prisoner delegate and the commander who does not move at all. I notice the red epaulettes of the new man's uniform and a red ribbon on his cap. A political commissar! A man from the GPU! Our delegate issues an order for an immediate gathering in the central square of all group leaders and all the officers.

I brought my team to our hut recommending not to go out while leaving the door open to catch some bits of what the meeting sounds like.

The barrack leaders were already gathering on the square and soon were there in full force. The commissar announces that this morning two prisoners had escaped. They will not get far! A search party is already on their way with the support of the entire population. There is a price on their heads. Those who take them, dead or alive, will pocket a premium offered by the regional government. And he insists that dead or alive they will come back here to your camp because they belong to your camp and anyone who had helped them will be executed! Then he called out all the barrack leaders. One does not answer: Major Friedrich. "What hut?" yelped the commissar. Our delegate told him and both depart. They return quickly. An NCO also missing the roll call. The commissar keeps ranting on. The delegate translated: "You German bastards! We will show you what it means to violate our rules! Immediate punishment for everyone, no soup tonight or tomorrow morning and the manager of the complex will double our work hours."

With that he left, still ranting and gesticulating, closely followed by the commander.

The delegate comes over to me:
- Tomorrow morning I will immediately inform the manager of the complex. This Friedrich guy, wasn't he in your hut in the beginning?
- Yes, but he wanted to run his own barrack. I did not have a good feeling about this guy and I'm glad he did not stay with us.
- So you did not know anything?
- No, not more than that.

The delegate had made his little investigation. This special status given to a prisoner was a Soviet invention to give a veneer of democracy to camp life. Some of the prisoner delegates behaved very well, others turned into real 'kapos', as in the Nazi camps.

*

The following day our guards had changed. In the past we would set off calmly for the mine supervised by only one of them. Now we had three of them harassing us constantly: "Dawai! Dawai!" Everyone seemed unnerved all day.

I immediately told Alexander of the changes that had taken place in the camp and the threats by the commissar of punishing all prisoners for the double escape:

- Last night and this morning we got no food or water. If this continues, our ability to work will take a hit because if you are hungry and thirsty, Alexander, you are good for nothing.

Karel barged into the office. He wanted to hear all the details. As I was talking he was overcome by a cold anger. He saw that the actions of any political commissar could screw up our arrangement and that production would be delayed well beyond September. He exchanged a few words with Alexander in Russian and then left.

- We will immediately deliver a good soup with bread for everyone. Meanwhile, we will serve you water.

- Thank you Alexander, we would like the soup before getting to work as our men are starving.

- I'm taking care of it. Afterwards everyone returns to work.

- All right, Alexander. We need to talk.

Quickly and generously served, the men returned to work and I was able to express my concern:

- What will happen to our relationship now? This is a political commissioner capable of anything. If he continues to punish the prisoners we can say goodbye to work.

Alexander did not know what to say. I went to encourage my team. Wilhelm and his Russian colleagues were hard at work to figure out how to strengthening the walls of the mine shaft to ease the movement of the elevator. All was well with the team that produced the beams. An additional motor from Germany will arrive tomorrow. I congratulated everyone and everywhere with the words: "Trust in God as I do and we will overcome this ordeal. Everything is arranged for the lunch soup."

After our shift we wearily made our way back to camp. The Commissar ordered each team to stand in front of the hut for a roll call. Still flanked by the commander and the deputy, he passed us in review. The two escapees were still missing. The commissar found every opportunity to throw his curses at us in Russian and when the delegate tried to translate he struck him half of the time at random. The scene seemed awfully strange. There was something more than a mere demonstration of gratuitous violence. He is too crazy, he is scared, I said to myself and I have come to know why.

The commander tried to put a word in while the commissar continued to shout in Russian at the top of his voice. This time, he let it be translated:

"You are all guilty! No soup tonight, tomorrow morning soup, but no bread. And nobody dares to leave his hut! The guards have orders to shoot without warning." I then said that my men will need to go to the latrine. Surprise! The commissar replied in German: "Then they will go before bed, accompanied by your barrack leader, same thing in the morning. If tomorrow one man missing, the responsible will be shot!" This man speaks German, but it is the German of the gutter. Where did he come from? What was his background? Why was he so hateful of us Germans? Was he perhaps one of those unfortunates that had suffered at the hands of the Gestapo?

In our hut a heavy silence hangs there:
- My dear comrades, the escapees cause us many problems. But tomorrow in the mine I'll take care of the situation. For tonight I propose two trips to the latrine, the first before going to sleep and the other in the morning.

Wilhelm comes to see me. He is a man of wisdom and I enjoy chatting with him. Calmly, we discussed our situation and how to approach Karel to solve our problems.

The the first light of day the delegate came for me to take me to the commander who was waiting, phone unplugged. He had three soups waiting for us:
- The commissar has left very early. I found a note in my predecessor's papers stating that you are in possession of a pouch that you wear on your neck and in which there are a cross and a

religious medal, plus a portfolio with family memories. Can I see these?

I could easily show them to him since I always kept them on me.
- If the commissar finds this note, he will ask you to give everything to him.

- I will never separate myself from my memories. They have become my talisman.

- You know he is quite able to kill you without much ado.

- Commander, I think you are an officer because you speak very good German, as the commissar does also but he speaks a very different kind of German. You understand perfectly what I am saying and I say that in case of a confrontation with this commissar I have nothing to fear: God will protect me.

Arriving at the mine, I took Alexander by the arm to give him a quick report. Karel comes running. I take it again from the beginning: our return to camp last night, the behavior of the commissar, his threats, his denying us food and water, the behavior of the morning guards. Karel listened patiently but he was visible boiling inside, not hiding that he will go and neutralize this commissar.

- We'll see you tonight. Alexander, double portion of soup and bread for lunch.

Alexander never had seen his boss in such a state. He told me that Karel had met with the new camp commander and had formed a good opinion of him, except that he was fully under the control of the commissar:

- Karel also telephoned the governor of Donetsk, a Ukrainian too. He made him aware of the situation. He learned that the commissar is originally from Germany and he is afraid of being unmasked perhaps as a former Gestapo man. He claims to have excellent connection in Moscow and with chief for the central GPU in Donetsk. The governor gave Karel discretion to do everything necessary to safeguard our collaboration. If mining work can start before the end of September there will be special bonuses and other benefits for everyone. Karel wants to be informed daily of what is happening in the camp.

*

In any event we hold all the right cards. On September 28 Karel announced that ten mines will be opened the next day ready for full production, in the presence of the governor. The prisoners are invited.

But that day in the camp the atmosphere was quite different. The commissar complained to the commander that the escapees were still not found. He was furious and as a direct consequence deprived us again of soup and bread from evening to morning. Instead he orders a triple ration of nighttime awakenings: everyone at attention in front of the hut to be counted and recounted.

In these conditions to get to the mine became a relief in every sense of the word. Once a hundred yards outside the camp our teams of prisoners took care of their bodily needs right and left.

Quickly, made aware of the state of affairs Karel phoned Alexander. As before, double portions of bread, water and soup. The governor should arrive around noon and his coming already had its effect: we can take a shower and we will even find paper in the latrine ('toilet paper' that came from torn cement bags). In addition, the opening of the mines will be declared holiday.

From afar we are see the inauguration ceremonies and the festivities. While the mines officials and the Ukrainian and Russian staff are partying with the governor, we are served a good vegetable soup with potatoes and two slices of white bread. Following the program we are invited to take a good nap!

By late afternoon I had informed Alexander of the recent measures taken by the commissar. Karel was still in a rage.

- That bastard, I'll have his skin!

- Karel, anger is a bad counselor! Make your decisions calmly, you know the Soviet system. Meanwhile let me do my thing and let us not lose contact with the commander.

In the wake of this beautiful inauguration the tyranny of Commissar had not abated.

On October 1, Alexander greeted me cheerfully:

- As of this morning my mine is in full swing. Look! Coal begins to come up in huge quantities.

- Congratulations! And elsewhere ?

- Five other mines already produce coal, others will at the latest in two days. We already have exceeded our norms. The mine managers, engineers and all the staff are happy and it is thanks to you.

- And the good work of the prisoners.

*

The commissar was waiting for us. It was obvious that he thinks he is now the actual camp commander. All work teams must wait outside the camp, except those of the escapees who are marched though the camp gates, followed by the commissar.

Very soon we hear the usual shouting in Russian and German, followed by a shot. The delegate is quick to make his report to the commander who, after a moment's reflection, relays the decisions by this GPU commissar: All teams must immediately return to their barracks, their officers in charge will gather in the central square. The Commissioner is waiting for them.

We are met with a disgusting scene of horror! On the square, three bodies lying on the ground, we see them right away. Two of them already seem like corpses. As for the third, I hardly recognize Friedrich. Tattered clothes, he is disfigured, one eye completely black, his ears shredded, his whole body covered with wounds. But he is still alive. Then the commissar in all his fury comes to us, pointing to the wretched soldier on the ground:

- This stuck-up bastard has confessed. Two prisoners helped him escape with his accomplice. I questioned the prisoners of his hut. Nobody wanted to talk. So I shot one of them just to set an example.

With a faint gesture of his hand Friedrich motioned to us to make us understand that none of this is true but seeing this the commissioner put a bullet in his leg. As his response to Friedrich's screams of pain the commissar kicks him in the side while shouting at us to fuck off and that no one will be allowed to leave their hut at night. No soup tonight or tomorrow morning. New orders will follow.

We complied in silence, frozen with terror. What would I tell my friends? Especially do not add despair to the horror! But everyone had certainly heard the gunshot. And no access to latrines? So I preferred to explain that this night new latrines would be built to replace the previous ones. Everyone would do his needs next to the house, being careful not to be seen by a guard.

- Is that all, Lieutenant? asked Wilhelm

-Yes that's it for now, except that there will be no soup or bread tonight or tomorrow morning. But we will have a double ration at the mine.

Wilhelm and Bernard had noticed that I had read the anxiety in the eyes of my comrades:

- Do not be afraid, I will do everything possible to protect you. For now fear reigns in the camp but for us freedom is in the mines. Say a prayer before going to sleep.

The night was pierced by several shots, probably aimed at prisoners that went out of their hut without taking enough precautions. Early morning the guards wake us up with their "Dawai! Dawai!" They take us out of the barracks to count us.

Our team's roll call showed that it was complete. Other barracks were not so lucky. Then the guards began to count again, they counted and recounted without stopping for a moment to yell at us. The commander and the delegate who came around eventually intervened to end this parody of organization that had no other purpose than to terrorize people and break their morale. The delegate told us that each team leader had to go to the central square where the commissar was waiting.

On seeing this sadistic murderer a feeling of disgust mixed with helplessness took possession of my whole being. Where the Friedrich and the two dead bodies were lying on the ground last night there was now only Friedrich but in what position! In the night, the commissar and his henchmen had dug a hole deep enough for the body of our comrade. Then they filled the hole, leaving only the head and neck uncovered. Now ants were all over his head going in and out of his nose and his ears without the slightest reaction from Friedrich. Posted next to his face was an inscription: "The slow death of an escaped prisoner of the Soviet Union." In order to prove that the former escapee was still alive the commissar cuts his cheek with his knife. Blood flows, a slight rattling sounds. With a sadistic grin, this torturer cleans the blade of his knife on Friedrich's skull. All this diabolical ceremony takes place in a dead silence! Then this monster informs us that the team of the escaped had spent the night building new latrines and that the bodies of other two escapees were already thrown into the old latrines.

- There is still enough room for this final escapee tomorrow night in your presence. The escapee's team will now return to the camp for different jobs. I hope I will unmask the other accomplice before tomorrow night. He may well be from another hut.

A sadistic smile accompanies these words full of heavy threats. The commander attended the macabre staging without making a sound.

Karel and all directors were meeting when we arrived at the mine. Karel organized a supply of water for everyone but also gave us the opportunity to take a shower. After that, we would be entitled to a double ration of soup and bread. A new cool shower, a piece of soap to rub the gums with your finger, then a semblance of a towel to dry.

What invaluable luxury!

The good hot soup gave my team mates the energy to get back to work. However, it could not erase a frightening mixture of sadness and fear in their eyes. And I? Fear? No, that left me long ago. I had only one thing in mind: to find ways to boost the morale of my comrades. How to do it? Alexander pulled me out of my thoughts:

- Come, let's see Karel.

He was not alone in his office. A commissar was there, too. The sight of his uniform made me cringe. Karel noticed my discomfort:

"Each director of a mining complex must accept the presence of a commissar to oversee the work and make reports to the headquarters of the GPU in Donetsk. I was lucky to get a Ukrainian comrade commissar who, in addition, speaks some German. He is aware of our relationship through which our mines could start on time. And, of course, the work is not finished yet. I await the delivery of ten full sets of new equipment tomorrow and I still need the services of your men for weeks to come. As soon as the cold weather will settle in it will become difficult to continue construction especially for the concrete foundations. Fortunately, we have gained a lot of good experience. On Wilhelm's advice we will build a wooden enclosure around the concrete foundations and the motors to insulate them from the cold. I had a brief telephone conversation with the camp commander. He told me that even he is frightened by you new commissar. He also told me that fifty-seven prisoners from the barracks of the escapees had nothing to eat or drink for five days. They had to work two nights in a row and are currently held in their hut with an armed guard outside the door."

I broke the silence that had followed Karel's report:

- Karel, tonight I will find the solution. God will guide me. Our commissar had his revenge, the escapees are dead. It's time he left the camp so that our teams can regain the same momentum and the same will to work for you.

The Ukrainian commissar added:

- Anyway, he better get out as soon as he can, otherwise we will come as a team this evening to arrest him. We do not like this type of comissars. In his hatred of everything German he went too far.

*

Back at the camp, the commander and the deputy ask us to form a compact column and makes us assemble on the central square. The commissar orders us to make a circle around the Friedrich's corpse. His face is half eaten by insects. With a theatrical and sadistic gesture, the commissar begins:
- You might imagine that he is not dead? We must make sure.
He draws his pistol and shots into the Friedrich's head, and then he spits in his face or whatever remained of it:
- This time, no doubt, he is dead.
We are stunned, some by horror, others by sheer hatred.
Then I look this criminal straight in the eyes and clearly see this man's own fear. A wave of cold fury goes through me through and through, and words come out of me in a supernatural calm:
- God taught us to love, to forgive those who trespass against us. You do not believe in God but you are very afraid. The big difference between you and me is that I met God and he said to me: do not worry, I'm on your side. It is a spiritual force that you do not have.
And while speaking I walk away from my comrades, towards him. He steps back, pistol in hand. Without any emotion in my voice, I tell him to lower his weapon because I have important things to tell him, but just you and me, alone. With his eyes he looks around - no more people to come to his rescue. We are alone, only me and him. I continue to walk with him.
"I know you're from Germany and we know what you have done there."
He starts to tremble.
"You can save yourself!"
He gives me a pleading look.

"Yes, yes, and here is the best advice I can give you: leave the camp right now. You know the way. If you have not left by 9pm a delegation of three Ukrainian commissars, together with the mine managers, will arrest you. They told me they do not like your type of goon and they have found out what you have done before coming here."

His gaze became fleeting. This ruthless man is paralyzed by his fear. Behind me, at fifty yards, I saw the commander and I asked him to call the commissar's driver to bring his car around because the commissar has completed his mission and wants to leave quickly. When the commissar comes back with his suitcase at his arm I said:
- If you leave immediately you will escape certain death.

I ask the commander to please call Karel to give him a very brief message: "We will see you tomorrow. The commissar is gone."

*

For the commander, the departure of the commissar was an enigma. How had I done it?
- Commander, with your permission, we will take our soup later in your office and we'll talk. But first we have important things to deal with. Everyone is waiting for us, I must speak to my comrades to reassure them and I want you to be with me.
- I follow you.

In the central square leaden silence, a tense atmosphere. I climb on a stool, the commander is with me:
- Comrades, God expelled the devil. It's not me, it's God who was with me. You all saw the way I dealt with the commissar. The words coming out of my mouth were not my own. It is God who dictated me gently as he did at Monte Cassino in May 1944. These words took the commissar off balance and dislodged all his aggressiveness and while I advanced towards him, he could only retreat. Fear had changed sides and when I asked him to drop his gun he did so. In half an hour we will have gotten got rid of this

criminal. I suggest we bury our unfortunate fellow Friedrich here. Sir, are you okay with this?

He nodded his consent. We quickly cleaned his already decaying body, dug a grave and deposited his body. While two volunteers were covering the grave I asked Bernard to make a cross. Wilhelm said, "It's already done." And he laid it on the grave. I stood in front of it and addressing myself to the officers, I said these words:

- Throughout the war we have buried many of our comrades. Rarely have we abandoned our dead, it was a point of honor for each of us. On the grave of the soldiers there was always a cross. Since we became prisoners of war many of our comrades died of hunger and thirst. A last prayer and the sign of the cross has always accompanied them. Today, thanks to our commander, we can properly bury a comrade and we'll think of all those we have lost their lives since the beginning of our captivity and who are buried somewhere in this vast country.

I made the sign of the cross:

- Dear Friedrich, you paid dearly your escape and you have also caused the death of your companion and a friend. May God grant them eternal peace. For you I ask forgiveness of our Lord Jesus Christ, that he forgives you your sins and grant you everlasting life. Dear comrades, together let us recite the "Our Father....."

On many faces I saw the tears flow and I thought how lucky we are that we still have tears to shed!

The commander was waiting for us to eat our soup, but I felt that my mission was not complete:

- Let's take some time before our evening meal. We are 1600 prisoners of war in this camp and we are working separately in the big mining complex. Today we attended the funeral of one of our comrades and we celebrated it in our religion. This allowed us to come together to learn more about us, respect and support us morally and spiritually. Believer or non-believer, Jesus reaches out to everyone, the door of his kingdom is always open. God exists and loves us infinitely. Especially we prisoners of war, with an uncertain future, need to have faith in God. Could we meet tomorrow evening to talk about it? Now take your soup because it will be particularly good, is it not, sir?

- Yes, certainly, he said, puzzled.

The officials of the barracks were not moving. The major who had never asked me anything asked if he could also invite friends from other barracks to the meeting that I had announced.

- Certainly. I will speak with the commander this evening.

It was my first one-to-one with the new commander. He wanted to talk of recent events, emphasizing the strong impression that the religious ceremony left with him and this incomparable fervor shown by all.

He was born near Moscow in 1922 and had never prayed or attended a church funeral. But his parents, even grandparents had attended Orthodox funerals conducted by a priest. Even after the communist revolution the Orthodox Church continued to serve its people. But after the death of Lenin Stalin took power and then any form of religion was outlawed, the priests were arrested and deported to Siberia, the churches destroyed or turned into warehouses:

"I have known the communist regime from my youth. My parents never stopped me from supporting Stalin's policies or to participate in the cult of his personality and in all events in honor of the Soviet Union. I fought in the patriotic war, as my father did and we contributed to the victory of Marshal Stalin. My father escaped the encirclement of the German army in 1941, he was in the war to the end and ended up a General. He is currently in Magdeburg, not far from Berlin. Maybe in two years I can join him. As you see, religion has never held any role in my life but this burial shook me. Your faith gives you an impressive force. You launched the idea of a meeting tomorrow night. I would like to participate."

- With pleasure sir.

- Ah! I believe that the delegate brings us our evening meal, the same as all prisoners. I invited him to share it with us.

In the background of our conversation, we heard the trucks starting their engines. The commander did not talk. He and the delegate were concerned for the sick prisoners still locked in the sick bay. Were they transportable?

- Yes sir, but in fact only half. The others are already dead or dying.

When I got there, it was terrible. Those still living are like the living dead, they no longer can stand up and keep demanding to drink, water, water! Fortunately, I planned three cans outside and empty boxes. With two other prisoners we organized the distribution. The poor guys gave off a terrible stench. We have sprayed them with water, especially the faces and heads. Then they were served a soup first and another an hour later with bread. There was something strange, some remained cloistered. They would not come out. Tomorrow I need a team of eight men to bury the dead, clean the hut and disinfect it. I dug two big graves. The survivors left in the trucks.

So that was it, that engine noise. The commander had to hire four trucks to transport the sick to a hospital for prisoners twenty miles away, but he was not optimistic:

- Our civilian hospitals lack medicines and supplies. For prisoners of war it is very simple, there are none. We were promised American and German drugs, but so far we have seen nothing.

*

Our daily routines could resume. In the morning we set off for work in rows of four, imitated in this by our neighboring teams. I was glad to see my example followed by others. It was a good start and it should convince everyone of the usefulness of this simple discipline. It is good for the morale of the men.

Alexander collared me as soon as we arrived at the mine and led me into the Karel's office. He was with the political commissar and three other mine managers, all Ukrainians. Everyone was eager to hear my story:

- As long as the commissar was in our camp, no one dared say a word. It was pure terror.

Then I told them everything from the beginning, day after day, until the final confrontation. When I finished, Karel spoke:

- I told you that Lieutenant Pappert is an extraordinary man. Thanks to him, our mines are the first in the region to produce coal for two weeks already.

I was a little embarrassed to get all this credit when so many of my comrades had made their own huge contributions. Karel shook my hand and made an appointment for later.

How long should we remain here? According to Alexander, at least several weeks but nothing was safe because now their work could continue without our involvement. As soon as the opportunity arose, I asked Karel:

- In principle, you will stay here another three or four weeks. But in other mining complexes there are the same problems, may be worse. Fear not, you will be notified in due time.

Meanwhile, we will eat a good soup together. It is already ordered. I'll call the commander to properly feed all your men because you should enjoy the same benefits with us. Our mines have far exceeded the work norms!

In the evening I was called to see the commander. I sensed reasonably good news. As he was my age we got along very well and did not need to beat around the bush to address the issue that concerned me above all: our future.

- I will most likely have to transfer you within two weeks to a camp in the north. There, the director of the mining complex has great problems. Maybe Karel has talked to you already?

- Yes, but only in vague terms. Are there already other prisoners there?

- Of course, but as the commanders are not allowed to communicate with each other I am hard pressed to tell you more. In any event you will be well treated here. Enjoy it! I do not know what awaits you in the other camp. Of course, all this must remain confidential.

So there was good news and not so good news. I immediately told my men the good news. Our hard work has paid off and everyone benefits: double rations of food, always good to take. One of the Stalingrad veterans said:

- Lieutenant, it is thanks to you, and thanks to the rapport you have been able to establish with those in charge that our lives as prisoners here have been completely transformed. We had lost hope but now we believe that with God's help we may be happy to see our homeland again.

- Tomorrow night I will organize a prayer meeting with all the leaders of our barracks and with any other comrades if they are interested. It would give me great pleasure if you would join us. Who is the youngest among us?

The young man who was with me on the train from Brno raised his hand:

- It could be me, I'm 18 and you taught me to pray, sir.

- You will be with me and when the time comes you will tell what you have seen and experienced, all of it. Do not forget that I am just one of your comrades and I am not a priest, but a simple believer since my birth. And now, good night to all.

*

How the conditions of our captivity had changed! Workdays went smoothly, and then returning to the camp for rest. But one detail bothered me. Karel had readily admitted that even though the prisoners were not experts in doing the mining work they had a much higher output than the Ukrainians. Would that not get us eventually into trouble with the Ukrainian miners? Karel shrugged:

- But no! What do you think? In the contrary, they are glad to benefit from the performance of the prisoners because of that they got an increase in their salary!

- So everything is fine?

The evening of the prayer meeting the commander confirmed his intention to attend. Kristof, our delegate, always rising to the occasion had four steel drums placed on the central square filled with wood. He had lit them just before the meeting as the evening air was already quite cool. We should bring a coat or some warm clothing.

When I showed up with my team, the place was already crowded. Almost the whole camp had responded to my invitation. In addition to the lights, Kristof had erected a small podium for two. The commander refused the chair that had offered to him. He preferred to remain standing. I thanked him for allowing us to hold this meeting.

Night began to fall. The four drums gave off a comfortable heat and some light as a symbol of serenity and hope. My throat was somewhat tight but I quickly regained confidence and I started:

"Comrades, we went through twelve years of Nazi terror. Each of us experienced it one way or another. An 'Austrian corporal' set Europe ablaze and into ruin. The world is not ready to forgive us for having submitted to a criminal regime that promised us a 'Thousand Year Empire' and endless prosperity for the German people. The end of the 1914-18 war had left the country in such disarray! Our country had become a rat race between communists, anarchists, socialists and political speculators of all sorts. The army of 100,000 soldiers allowed us by the Versailles Treaty became the basis for a future army dominated by the Prussian nobility. They were hoping for a Bismarck to get rid of the injustices of the Versailles Treaty and build a new Germany, but instead they got an Austrian corporal. You all know what happened next.

Your parents and many of you have accepted the new Nazi policies and their simplistic slogans. Hitler's new 'Cult of Providence' would replace our Christian traditions. Faith in God? Wherever it was proclaimed it was branded as reactionary, something to be removed from the lives of people. How many believers are still among you? You, the officers, you have received orders and executed them. Have you thought for one moment that these orders were often unscrupulous and utterly contrary to our morality? The war is over, the time has come to speak our conscience. I wanted this meeting because I saw that you feel helpless as prisoners. You did not understand that faith in God is for us a spiritual force that protects us from despair, the 'let us die' attitude. Like you, I have experienced the destructive power of the Nazis. I was born into a Catholic family and always I remained a man of faith. In 1942, I was barely 17 years old!"

From there I proceeded with the story of my life as a soldier, the Monte Cassino battles, my decorations, my meeting with the SS captain, the Potsdam officers school, my training of new recruits of the Home Guard, my meeting with the Nazi Schörner, and on 8 May 1945, the last shelling from the T-34, my prayer, the death of my comrades, and the miracle of my coming out of this alive.

My memories of my campaigns were not those of a veteran flaunting his exploits and the good times of war. No, what I wanted was a constant reminder why and how I could go through all these trial and tribulations. There was a single explanation: my faith in God. Not only my faith but also confessing to it whatever the circumstances. I was always ready to practice my religion while in the military, despite the objections of my superiors. I went to Mass whenever it was celebrated. Even to the SS captain I freely stated that I was a believer and he bowed to my determination. He became my protector!

All my stories were meant to bring religious feelings up in my fellow prisoners, to protect the living and respect the dead and to pray for them. That's what I wanted to convey to my audience: the importance of faith in God and his son Jesus Christ and the Virgin Mary, mother of God. How could I best perform this duty?

I called on the young soldier from Brno and asked to explain how he became a believer himself. His explanations were not those of an intellectual, they had the simplicity and sincerity of which everyone's heart is capable. We were reliving the martyrdom of the prisoners on the train, the many dead, with fear everywhere, and my desperate attempts to give them courage to live. He ended in tears and simply said, "Thank God. I became a happy man."

I again challenged the audience: "Have others of you discovered or rediscovered your faith?" Bernard, both of the men from Stalingrad, Wilhelm and virtually all of my team came forward. What a joy!

"I pray to God to grant happiness to you all. God exists and loves us infinitely. And when you are in very difficult situations, without hope, pray with all your heart and ask God and his son Jesus Christ and the Virgin Mary to help you in these very difficult times. God will never abandon someone who has opened his heart and his soul to Him. Soon winter will come and we do not know what awaits us, perhaps the worst time of our lives. Our two comrades in Stalingrad have been there. Now they know that only faith in God and our sincere prayers can give us the strength to go forward, not to give in. And when sickness and death threaten us, just pray: "Holy Mary, mother of God, pray for us sinners now and at the hour of our death. Amen." We want to live and we know that God will not abandon us. We want to overcome fear through prayer. So do not forget a little prayer, a thought that takes you to God and makes you happy.

And if you have the happiness to escape from captivity and regain your family, contact your parish, tell about your reunion with God in 1945 in a prison camp in the Donbass coal mines. You will be invited to some sessions of catechism and to receive your baptism. And when you attend your first Mass, then your first communion, you will hear the priest's words: "Lord, I am not worthy to receive you but only say the word and I shall be healed." Repeat to yourself pray intensely receiving the wafer from the priest's hand, accompanied by the words: "The body of Christ." You will feel the healing of your soul and great joy will come to you. It is the joy of living that will accompany you in your new life as Catholic."

I concluded with these words: "May God Almighty bless us now and forever. In the name of the Father, the Son and the Holy Spirit, Amen." Everyone crossed himself at the same time, including the commander.

"A final word to the leaders of the barracks: when we leave the camp put yourself in line and when passing the commander give him the military salute. This also will give courage to your comrades, lift your spirits, and joy is part of our discipline.

By the way, I learned that soon the health service will come for the usual examinations. Tomorrow we will go to the mine as usual in rows. In addition, this evening we receive coats, because the cold weather arrives. I wish you a good night."

*

CHAPTER 9

Another Camp, another Mine

The next two days passed without a hitch. Our cooperation with the mines managers and their staff was perfect. We would have liked this to continue for long. But on the third night the commander called me to his office.

With a worried look he announced out of the blue that half of our camp, specifically all professionals, will be transferred to another camp in the north of Donbass. My team is part of the transfer.

- You will take command of all these fourteen teams of prisoners. I will give you a message in Russian that you hand in person to your new complex director. The prisoners who remain will continue to work in the mines here. I do not deny that the change will not be easy.

- Karel, why do you tell me all this?

- Our director called to convey his thanks to you. He and the other directors will never forget you. He wishes you good luck.

- Our delegate is about to contact all barrack heads to come to my office after the evening meal.

These men are coming at once. It was getting cold and we put on our worn coats that were missing several buttons. Accompanied by the delegate, the commander repeated what he had told me. Then he handed a list to the delegate who called out each team. The commander spoke again:

- Tonight we will distribute winter headgear, old Red Army fur hats, but they are clean, warm and cover the neck and face. I asked Lieutenant Pappert to assume command of all fourteen teams. He will be in charge of all contact with the head of your new mining complex.

In his office the commander gave me a message for the director of the new complex. Meanwhile we had already received our 'new' headgear. I grabbed the first one and put it on my head. Impeccable. It was true that it protected you well from the cold.

My men were anxiously awaiting me.

- Lieutenant, you have a funny hat on your head!

The delegate distributed them to the others and a sort of fitting session began. At the end we all looked just like Red Army soldiers.

I told them about the program for the next days which does not meet with any enthusiasm. This is understandable. Now they have settled into our routine here and had found their bearings. Naturally, they would not see this change in a positive light. They say that they have more to lose than to gain from it.

- Listen, anyway, we should have expected to change our workplace and camp more than once. This is the fate of us prisoners of war in the Soviet Union. This is a huge country and we will have to help fix whatever the German army had destroyed in retreating. Remember our orders to leave nothing behind but scorched earth? We may have very hard times in the future but never lose your faith in God. He alone can help you. Tomorrow we leave together on a journey into the unknown. It's the winter that we have to fear most. Say a little prayer before you go to sleep.

I was among the first to fall asleep.

Around 7am all the men were awake. The rumor mill had started to turn. "Lieutenant, do you have an idea about our future workplace? Is this an area like here? And what about the the camp commander? How are the mines? And how are the barracks?" I was assailed by a thousand questions.

- I understand you are worried but I do not know more than I told you. Even the commander knows no more, he is 23, he is a lieutenant like me and he will probably be appointed to another camp in the coming weeks. Why? Just because here he had done too many things contrary to Communist doctrine and he is probably considered a danger to the army. It is the Soviet system. They keep their officials in a permanent state of insecurity about their fate and they think of nothing else. So do not complain and keep your courage so that we may see our homeland again. Another tip: after the soup, drink water, lots of water, because here it is clean. During the trip, I do not think we will have many opportunities to quench our thirst.

We left around 9am. In each truck were two young guards who did not speak a word of German. The road was bad. We could not go faster than perhaps 20mph but without a stop. Finally our new camp was in sight. What time was it? One of the guards showed me his watch: 2pm. We must have travelled about 60 miles. The landscape was dotted with mines and it was much colder. No commander was there to welcome us to our new 'home' but a new prisoners delegate stood at the gate.

He was a Pole from Karlowitz who spoke German and Russian. Like his father, he had worked in the mines. He was only 19 when the Germans invaded Poland and had not yet been drafted into the Polish army. In 1943 he had been drafted into the Wehrmacht, classified as 'generic German'. In 1944 he was captured by the Red Army and trained as a propagandist, charged with encouraging

German soldiers to desert. At our arrival his role was to give us the instructions of the commander and assign us to our barracks.

- I'm a lieutenant and I will take charge of this one if you agree.

- No objections. Anyway, in an hour the commander wants a meeting with all team leaders.

The barracks were designed to house a hundred prisoners each. In the midst of our own a coal stove was supposed to create a 'warm' atmosphere! A smell of chlorine told us that the barracks had been disinfected. There were no mattresses but the floor was clean. I settled near the door and my team quickly gathered around me, Wilhelm, Bernard and others. I sensed fear in the prisoners.

- Right now everything is new to us, we are confused and that is normal. Trust yourself and trust me. All team leaders are summoned to the commander for a first meeting. After my return I can probably tell you more.

The delegate came for me later. He had only been here for two days and was as new as we are. He would get to know the 'lay of the land' for the benefit of all of us.

The commander was waiting for us. The delegate translated his orders:

- The prisoners that arrived today must report immediately to the health service. The showers are located right next door.

- Then find the new soup kitchen.

- Tomorrow morning, soup at 7 am and departure for the mine at 8pm. The new team leaders must report to the director of the complex.

- The older ones will do their chores as usual.

- Six latrines are installed outside the camp, guarded day and night. There are signs showing the way. Avoid hanging around there, do not talk to each other. Do your needs and go back quickly because the guards are 'trigger-happy'. That's all for today.

I asked my men to leave their coats to mark their place and follow me to the health service. One of them told us to take a quick shower and to appear before the commission in our 'birthday suit'. As I was undressing myself I hid my 'talisman' and my wallet under my clothes. A quick shower with soap, then a small piece of cloth to dry and then shoo! back outside. The head of the commission took our information. Then the shaving session with a nurse and we dressed and returned to our hut shivering. We found our way to the kitchen. The soup was warm but thin, with a slice of bread.

*

It took an hour of brisk walking to get to the mine. I imagined that they would lead us to the mines manager but it was only to a translator who gave us our program in German. All this was unclear. I asked to see the manager.

His office was 200 yards away. I salute and request a private conversation because I guess he speaks German like all officers. Without comment he turns to his translator and I give him the message from my former commander. He reads and rereads then places a call. Soon after four people arrive. They are the mine managers. As he speaks in Russian, I interrupt immediately:

- As a military veteran you must have learned to speak German?

Indeed, they all understood and spoke enough German. Three of them were Ukrainians, one was the overall director. I then described the situation that we found mid-July in our previous mining complex:

- The close collaboration between mine management and us prisoners of war allowed the mining complex to exceed the norms by the end of three months and everyone benefited.

I had uttered the magic word: "the norms". Guaranteed effect.

- When we left there the manager told me something about your complex, that you have many difficulties to run the mines. It would be useful to immediately organize a meeting with your chief engineer and my specialists. This would allow us to establish a rational work plan to tackle the problems in order of priorities.

I left the office and went for Wilhelm, Bernard and others. The director also asked four more people to come to his office where a large map of the complex was spread out in front of us. This mine was twice as big as the one we left. Logically, there should be twice as many prisoners.

- Nothing works here, lamented the director. Our pumping engines constantly break down, the water is not drained from the mine shafts. The support beams are too short. We have five mines here to bring up to speed. Our engineers have laid foundations for three but when the big elevator motors arrived they found that the bolts were not consistent. We are unable to mount the engines. A real disaster.

- Who is responsible?

- Our engineers. We, the directors know nothing about construction.

- How many engineers do you have for complex?

- Three teams of four engineers and two chief engineers.

- I see, it was like our old place of work. Do you have a chief engineer who speaks German and possibly knows the technical terms?

One of the three chief engineer raised his hand.

- You immediately begin working with Wilhelm, one of our engineers. Bernard will be responsible for the pumping engines and there will be a specialist for concrete work. Whoever is responsible for the engine should show Bernard the pump motors. While my men make a first assessment of the situation, I would like to speak with the manager and the directors of the mines.

The director sent everyone to work and I remained alone with him:

- I watched you. You are a man with initiative and good thinking, I fully trust you.

- Thank you, Director, you will see the difference between the training of our specialists and yours. We will do good work together.

I felt I could push my luck. The opportunity was good to talk about camp life and how to improve it:

- We are in mid-October, it's getting cold, our men are still in their summer clothes, except for old coats and the fur caps. It is imperative to get warmer clothes, otherwise they will get sick and then they cannot give you the work you expect from them. We also need some heat in our barracks. There are stoves but no coal. The food is insufficient. How can you expect good work from the prisoners when they are cold with an empty stomach? Even here it will be necessary to make some fire outside to keep warm. Otherwise we will not make progress.

The director noted my requests. He had already given instructions by telephone and gave the order to prepare hot soup for lunch for all our teams. It would be served around a fire.

- Now I will call your camp commander.

He was speaking in Russian. I do not understand this language but it did not prevent me from noticing that the discussion was stormy. The commander was reluctant to the point that the director suddenly raised his voice, struck his fist on the table and had to start issuing threats. On the phone I could hear the commander saying "da, da da" and more "da".

With a triumphant smile, the director told me that tonight or at the latest tomorrow night we would have warmer clothes and that he would try to improve the evening meal and but it would depend on the results of our work. Well, here we are: give and take.

- Anyway, what is your name?
- Boris, call me Boris, it's easier.

With Boris' agreement my specialists completed their first inspection tour and we can make them start into their new work environment.

While waiting for them I thought, with a good dose of self-confidence, I could continue to deal with our new superiors even from my weak position as a prisoner of war. It is true that I was riding on our successes in the southern complex and, thank God, on the reputation of my comrades who were true professionals that the managers of other mines would not have at their disposal. Again, this would be our chance to make ourselves indispensible, with our hope for improved food and work conditions.

Wilhelm, Bernard and the concrete specialist arrived. I asked them for a first report. Boris just listened. Wilhelm began by explaining that three concrete foundations were unusable:

- I saw some prisoners struggling to demolish the bases with medieval tools. They have already worked at it for two weeks and did not make any progress. We must break up the top layer of the foundations and then rebuild it for the exact dimensions to install the bolts.

Boris thought: I will immediately give orders to demolish the base.

With a glance, I encouraged Wilhelm to continue:

- I know someone who might be helpful. He belonged to the army engineers and is specialized in blasting.

- Trust us. My men know their stuff. Just ask your engineers to listen to them and help them find the hardware. Wilhelm, take care of the foundation problem with the chief engineer. Bernard, go to work with your team to solve the engine problem.

- Aye sir.

Before the end of the day the motors are running and Bernard had trained other technical teams. A few days later the mining complex was teeming with activity. Our teams had taken over the production of beams. If all went well the first mines could begin to produce coal in two to three weeks. Boris was more than satisfied:

- You Germans are the best because of your training.

*

But at the camp no good vibes were passing between the commander and me. The evening meal was not any better, neither was the bread. The water in large containers definitely had a funny taste.

Two days later the stink of diarrhea from several of my men, including me. I immediately informed the delegate. Thirty of us were no longer able to move. The next morning we were put in another hut with some of those who still could digest the soup without problems. Three days later the health service man came to check us and declared us fit to get back to work. The nurse wanted to warn me that our new camp commander was known for his brutality. It was always good to know but what could we do about it?.

We had to void literally on the spot. No more appetite, but a terrible thirst. With my experience in the transit camp I asked our representative to prepare us slices of charred bread. It was useless, the commander had already chartered two trucks to transport us to a prisoner hospital ten miles away.

In this hospital we were put on mattresses and again I asked a nurse if you could get burnt toast and completely dehydrated I asked for water. The nurse, very young, came back with a man in a white coat, speaking a little German who told me immediately that they had no more drugs but the charred slices of bread would indeed be a very good remedy against diarrhea. They were going to make some for us.

The bread arrived, one slice of charred bread per person. With my mouth completely dry it was very difficult to chew the infamous charcoal and it really was going down very painfully. The nurse had distributed a little water in small tin cans. I did not know all these prisoners but I had to warn them:

"Do not drink water, it's very dangerous! You will never heal!" Nothing doing. More than half were chasing their bread with water. Those around me had heard me and continued to swallow the dry bread-coal. It was hard, very hard. Three days later, one morning we had a spoon of thick porridge and another slice of charred bread. I prayed to Our Lady to help me.

For those who did not eat charcoal, diarrhea flared up and this time they were losing blood. The nurses transferred them to another room to let them die.

The next morning we were put in another hut with those who could digest the soup without problems. Three days later the health guy came back and after a cursory examination declared us good to go back to work. Again the nurse wanted to warn me that our new camp commander was known for his brutality. This was always good to know but now what?

*

CHAPTER 10

Finding the True Meaning of Christmas

Is there a threshold beyond which the physical and moral suffering ceases to exist? Should I have to exceed these limits to find out? I did not want to ask these questions, but I think I have experienced it as a test from the Lord.

Acute dysentery led me to the hospital so that there would be no long term health consequences. I was no longer in the camp where I had established good relations with the commander. I had been sent to Camp No. 367 in northern Donbass and it had a bad reputation.

It was towards the end of October and it was already very cold. As an officer I was put in charge of 400 prisoners. At 7 in the morning we left the camp and walked a mile or so to the 'Lenin' mine where we worked until 6pm.

On the way back we carried several pieces of coal in our pockets that the guards allowed us to take with us for the stove in the midst of our barracks. As there were still some patients there they already had prepared a little fire and we entered a vaguely warm room.

In late November a terrible cold wave descended on the region with lots of snow. We put on our extra clothes, felt boots, pointed caps, fur, always from old stocks of the Red Army. These outfits had gone through a lot already and it was not a nice picture, torn at many places, the coats often without buttons. Whatever! In the camp like everywhere, sewing was done with wire or other left over scraps. Any additional layers were welcome to cope with this infernal cold.

Given the decay of our physical strength walking in the snow took us more time. To avoid losing work efficiency the Russians decided to transport us in military trucks.

*

One morning we started at 7am as always, after our so-called vegetable soup. It would take someone very clever to find many traces of vegetables in this water! We chewed half of our bread ration, the other half we kept for the soup at lunch which was no better. I thought of our soups in our previous camps.

The guards had changed. They made liberal use of rifle butts to make us faster climbing into the trucks!

I had met a Frenchman from Sarreguemines that had been captured last February. He was one of those unfortunate Alsatians that been conscripted into the German army. Like many of his compatriots he continued to demand his repatriation to France. In vain. His name was Edmond and was 22. He was a brave man, often ready to come to the defense of other prisoners. He argued loudly about his French nationality.

As he climbed into the truck he received a violent blow in the back which cause him to cry out in pain. He was about to fight back but I dissuaded him. For me it was clear: this guard, a real brute, was only waiting for a sign of rebellion to bring him down for good. The atmosphere is very tense.

Arriving at the mine we learned that a pump had broken down. This means that a layer of black mud was waiting for us at the bottom of the mine. We'll have to wade in there for hours. As we came down in the elevator we removed some of our clothes to keep them dry. No use. After several hours of very hard work we were soaked to the skin and so were the clothes we had tried to keep dry.

On the one hand we were anxious that this day would end but on the other hand we feared what we would find at the top of the mine shaft. This fear was not imaginary. Once at the surface we could hardly breathe under the onslaught of the biting icy wind. One thought only: run as fast as you can to the trucks and then back to our barracks.

But the brutes that surround us have something else in mind. In their drunken stupor, with hatred written all over their faces they are determined to make us suffer, just for their entertainment. I see this coming. Knowing the character of Edmond I catch him immediately to tell him to shut up because of the big risk.

The sinister comedy begins with an order. We have to empty our pockets and lay down the coals. Then, one by one, the prisoners have to march between two guards who check if the pockets are empty. My turn comes. I had my piece of bread from the morning, completely frozen. The guard laughs when he discovers it and let me go. A prisoner who believed he could conceal a bit of coal is immediately beaten over and over with sticks and kicked until he collapses in the snow. And as he does not come up fast enough, here they go again. Those who still have coal in pockets get rid of them quickly and discreetly.

After this first scene the guards ordered us to line up as usual for a head count which should have been a formality. We were 88 prisoners in the morning, the same as in the evening. Besides we have already been counted by our four Russian foremen.

Totally drunk, a guard nevertheless wants a recount. Coming close to the end he loses the thread, gets tangled, does not know where he is. Our wet clothes stiffen as they freeze in the icy wind. At this rate we'll die of the cold. Something needs to be done. I start to do some arm and leg movements. Edmond yells: "Move, guys! Otherwise we will die on the spot!"

The nurse was right by putting me on guard against the commander. He picks on us immediately on arrival, foaming with rage. He knows the reason for the delay but he takes it out on us! Double rations cut out and we finally enter the barracks totally exhausted.

We felt like children who had momentarily escaped their tormentors. The brief moment of being in a safe haven and a little heat was quickly replaced by anxiety. There is virtually no coal. The whole hut will soon again be engulfed in this infernal cold. The night is going to be terrible. I prayed, "Lord, do not abandon us. Lady, protect us."

Those who still have the strength attempt to remove their frozen clothes. The weaker do not even attempt to change.. They stretch out on the floor waiting for death. They gave up, broken, suffering. Suddenly the door opens. It is the prisoner delegate. Without real power, however, his job is to deceive the representatives of the Red Cross which, according to rumors, began to inspect the camps in search of civilians rounded up by the Russians at the end of the war and thrown in with POWs.

Our delegate and several men have their arms full of clothes. They also have coal and make us a sign to remain quiet. All the guards are in a meeting with the commander and they took advantage of their absence to bring us some comfort. They take our wet clothes and leave. We help the weak to undress and change into dry clothes to sleep on their mattress without a blanket. I thanked our Lord Jesus Christ and the Virgin Mary for saving us.

Usually after coming back from the mine and the distribution of soup there is always some moment of physical and spiritual recovery. All hells have their intermissions, some quiet moments where the only distraction is to chat with the unfortunates. And what were we talking about? What was the single most important subject? The food! Again and again the food, an inexhaustible subject. All the days of my captivity, I never heard anyone talk about girls or love as all memories of pleasure had flown out of the heart and body of the thousands of men brought down by hunger. We spent time to make us salivate at the memory of the good things we had eaten, that we hope we would eat again one of these days.

But that night the quiet of a mortuary had descended on us. Even Edmund, who I had dubbed the eternal revolutionary was silent. The silence was not even relieved by the loud snoring of some. Normally, the neighbors would have shaken them to stop but now nothing, not the slightest reaction.

I knelt down to watch this heap of tired humanity, or what was left of it. The light was low, three bare bulbs on all night. I saw these dirty silhouettes blackened by the mining mud, these ghostly faces, burnt out, a herd of undead that no longer reacted to the sound of barking guard dogs. Deprived of our meager evening meal, living for weeks in this camp of terror made us into human beings that no longer really existed. Which of these men was still able to act, to make a decision or simply gather his thoughts?

I wanted to talk to Edmond but he was sleeping. So I was just watching him. I rebooted the stove and I lay down under one of the coats lent by our comrades. Before falling asleep I said my daily prayer and thought about my father, intensely. I remembered his words: "My son, never forget that we are waiting for your return, even if you only return to us as skin and bones, but alive!" I saw my mother, she traced the cross on my forehead, fingers wet with holy water. I saw her eyes full of love and hope, and I swore to myself that I will not let myself be cut down by these dogs. I thought in this country a man was not worth much, they were certainly more humane to their cattle than to us. Then I fell into a deep sleep.

A punch in the back woke me up. Edmond struggled against a nightmare. I shake him, he opens his eyes, mumbled a few words in French that I did not understand.

- Edmond! Do you recognize me ? It's me, your friend Aloÿs, your neighbor.

He stares at me blankly. It takes him several minutes to be himself again.

- I had a nightmare. I was fighting against the Bolsheviks and I felt I was going to lose. It was terrible! Poor Edmond, for the moment they are the ones who beat us!

Edmond, bewildered, was not quite himself again. By placing my hand on his forehead I knew he had a high fever. He was probably not the only one. Plaintive groans went up from everywhere. My comrades' sleep was restless, filled with feverish nightmares. Anxiety gripped me. What were we to become? As a stopgap, I put a wet rag on Edmond's forefront, another on his chest, hoping the fever would subside. What else can I do?

It was an oppressive night without benchmarks. What time could it be? Poor sleep is breaking down the perception of time. Get out of the barracks? Totally impossible. Usually we hear the guards patrolling with their dogs. They had to wake us up two or three times, anytime, for anything. They brawled, exciting their dogs. Edmond finally goes back to sleep. I got up to put some coal in the stove but another prisoner had thought of it already. Before I go back to sleep, I sent a final prayer to my guardian angel.

The day finally came up.

- Hello comrades! I present you the new commissar, deputy commanding general of the military district and his lieutenant, your new commander for the camp 367. The prisoner delegate has shouted out this sentence. Still stunned by fatigue, I open my eyes and make out two officers, a commissar of the GPU and a military man.

In a perfect German the commissar informs us that the four Russian foremen, managers of our group made a statement about the incidents of the previous day. Consequently our camp commander was immediately placed under arrest and replaced by a new commander with all new the guards. From now on this will be a military detachment under the responsibility of the lieutenant who became head of the camp. Our group stays at rest today. "Who is responsible for this hut?" inquires the Commissar.

I'm getting up. Now or never :

"Comrade Commissar, I was appointed head of this group by the former commander. As an officer with the rank of lieutenant in the German army I accepted this responsibility but I never had the right nor the opportunity to speak to the commander. We are prisoners of war and we submit to the camp rules. But we are men. We do not ask much. Respect us as human beings! Look at my comrades. What a state they are in! Last night was not the first time he has deprived us of our thin soup and our bread ration. How can we have the strength to work? We have reached our limits and in the stench of this shit, half of my comrades have passed these limits. They will die, Comrade Commissar, die!"

To say these words I had to muster all my strength. My legs gave way, I stumble, I fall. The Commissar rushes to try to support me. Before falling, I still have the strength to say: "Please, hurry, a doctor ..."

And I lost consciousness.

When I woke up I was lying in my usual place. Someone woke me from my sleep to make me eat a little. He handed me the old tin can which we used as a dish since my arrival in Russia, plate, cup, pot, it served as all that.

A soup! I quickly searched for my spoon, my last relic from the German army. Sharpened on one side, this rusty blade still had not seen the color of sausage! Could it be, was this a hallucination? On the surface of the soup floated cabbage leaves, some pieces of potato and even, incredible, waves of meat filaments! Besides a double ration of bread was waiting for me, real bread, not this rotten 'ersatz' stuff. It was so unexpected I thought myself transported to paradise.

A glance around me was enough to bring back the sordid realities. No, I was not in paradise! It was hell unchanged from the barracks. Even after so many years I find it distasteful to talk about "pig shit" but to be frank, our hut did stink of shit. The prisoners, degraded, reduced to the level of caged animals, could not go out at night to go to the latrine. How to do our needs? Where to relieve ourselves? At the back of the hut, into an old tub that had to be emptied every morning and dumped into the open latrines. I had never seen anything like it in any prison camp, such a morbid desire to completely break us, to cancel the last natural resistance of men to be pushed beyond the bearable just to see us die like a beast!

Stink or not, I swallowed this dream soup and swallowed all my pain. I felt better. I resumed walking slowly. The stranger who had served me the meal was still watching me, sitting in front of me. Now he offered me an extra ration! My eyes would express such disbelief that the man began to explain the reasons for this 'opulence'.

He was part of a group of prisoners from the camp 364. He and his comrades had brought food to prepare a soup there, and had seen that in our 'kitchen' there was absolutely nothing. The former commander diverted the better part of our rations for his own benefit and for his friends, black market operators. All we got were the 'crumbs that fell off his table'.

- Who sent you here?
- Your new commander requested it.

In addition to the team that had prepared the soup, another was at work with the order to clean and disinfect he barracks and to replace the rotten and stinking mattresses. I figured then we would move to another hut to wash and to be shaved from head to foot and then to be disinfected prior to receiving clean clothes. I was dreading this meeting. I knew that it was very painful. Literally eaten by lice our skin was dotted with festering scabs and multiple small open wounds. The razor would scorch everything in its path and, of course, there was no hope for sympathy from the 'nurses'. They operated, without qualms, the disinfectant burning the skin. The rest of the program was the 'medical examination' consisting of the usual pinching of our buttocks.

We were still in this pigsty but once I had the good soup there was renewed hope for a change. I took advantage of this respite to check: many prisoners of our barracks were no longer there, the rest in a sorry state. Some did not even have the strength to eat. My friend Edmond had disappeared.

Die here, or die in the hospital, being thrown into a hole, naked after the obligatory salvaging of clothes. Die and be buried like a dog! At the beginning of our captivity I had to bury comrades. We still had tears to shed, even the strength for a quick prayer. But today we had no more tears, no more prayers, no more words, we were more than dead! My God, my God, what were we now?

Determined to glean some news, I get up from my mattress. That's when our delegate rushed in: "I'm coming for you, the commander wants to see you. Quickly he throws his own coat over my shoulders and puts a fur cap on my head. Walking through the crisp snow I become aware of the temperature: at least 30 degrees below zero! This is like Siberia! My chest and back are hurting with each breath.

The delegate sums up the latest events of this morning after my call for help and my fainting. The political commissar immediately phoned headquarters. Two trucks arrived with doctors and medical personnel on board. 44 prisoners of our barracks were evacuated and about thirty others, all taken to a hospital which is already full. Edmond must be among them. And it's not over. Many other prisoners should be admitted to the emergency room or they'll die here. We can not even dig a mass grave because the earth is frozen like a block of stone!

With my head full of these gloomy visions, the delegate and I arrive at the new commander. He is not alone. The commissar and two other officers are with him. The commissar translated the testimony of the four Russian foremen and he asks me to sign as the officer responsible for our barrack. I could add what happened after the shooting but I prefer to stick to a simple signature. The four foremen were brave enough to dare to make this statement. My thoughts are with these men. One of them was an engineer.

Relations with them remained human. Despite the food rationing that even applied to the civilian population and in spite of the prohibition by our guards these foremen quietly used to, every so often, slip us a piece of bread, a baked potato or an onion.

I knew that our brigade was required to produce a certain amount of coal daily. With our men getting weaker by the day and the number of sick increasing it became increasingly difficult to meet the poduction quotas. Our foremen were getting nervous, they threatened us with a report to the commander. They were fully accountable and they were not immune to punishment, even being sent to a forced labor camp. I had enough experience with prison camps to know that they were right to be afraid. But what should we do

I asked them:
- Who controls the quantities of coal to be brought up?
- We send the production reports to the Mine administration who compares us to the industry standard and to the average of the Donbass mines. Each month the excess over the standard entitles the directors and managers to get a bonus and extra food stamps, including us.
- And on the surface?
- On the surface, there is no control because it is the prisoners that carry the coal to the cars.
- So it's simple. Our daily production is based on so many cubic yards made by a brigade of 100 miners. If we are only 90 or 85, the standard drops 10 or 15%. Therefore, you write your report based on the decline of available labor and occasionally you exceed the standards for a premium.

The supervisors agree without adding a word. A week later, I learned from one of the mines engineers that they had received congratulations from management for our production success. They had not taken long to understand how to beat the system.

Outside, reality quickly caught up with me. The cold was less felt but the pain in my chest increased. I began to cough. From there, I became increasingly disoriented. There was a medical examination. I see myself in a cold shower, someone soaped my back, wiped me with indescribable stuff, a nurse began shaving, and then ... a big black hole.

*

When I came back to myself I was in a bed, shivering and coughing among forty other beds and many patients, maybe more, maybe less, in a 'hospital' for prisoners. I was in a daze, distinguishing faintly things around me with images parading in my mind before getting settled in. Two white coats, a mature woman, another a bit younger. They lean towards me with a black and hard look. I hear Russian, they take my temperature, still speak, examine me. The older looks at me and it's like she said "Poor devil, you're screwed." In the eyes of the younger was sadness, however, hope is not turned off yet. At least that is what I believe. She strokes my forehead and my cheek. She just gives me what I have been deprived of for so long! In this world of despair, noise and death, there are still people who know how to convey a sense of love and peace. They are able to stop time with a simple gesture. It is like magic.

Later, the blonde nurse returns. She makes me take a powder in a cup of hot water, a vaguely tinted tea. It was as if I were in pieces with pain throughout my body and I was coughing more and more. Fever dominated me completely, I was boiling and yet so cold.

The next few days passed in dazed confusion. I had lost lucidity. Later, the nurse told me about the terrible pneumonia that was slaying me with very high fever spikes. Every morning the doctor, with her hard look, was surprised to find me still alive.

The young nurse spoke enough German. She had studied it at school and at university like many Russians. She was hired as a nurse along with the doctor and three other nurses to care for 600 patients. Half of the patients came out more or less healed, the others ... peace to their souls.

The hospital lacked everything. The inventory was simple: there were three thermometers and a perpetual shortage of dressings, medicines other medical supplies.

*

One morning my fever has miraculously fallen. I almost left this life. When I opened my eyes I looked at the ceiling and then everything around me without understanding why the scene had changed. It was not that the decor had changed but I was looking at everything like a newborn. I felt filled with a feeling of happiness, the happiness to be alive and to be aware of it. With all my soul, I gave thanks: "Thank you! Thank you Holy Virgin, Mother of God Jesus Christ, you protected me! My God, I believe in you, you're still so close to me. And my 'guardian angel'? Where is she?" The door opened and I saw her, dressed all in white, enveloping me with her angelic look. It was the nurse.

She runs towards my bed, crying: "It's a miracle! He's alive!" She immediately calls the doctor: "Olga! Olga! Come quickly! A miracle!" The doctor feels my pulse, puts her hand on my forehead, nods and says in German to the nurse, "Yes, yes, for me he was dead." Then she turns away.

- What day is it ?
- December 9, replies the nurse.

My birthday! Back to life on my birthday, and not just any birthday but 21 years! As if I was born a second time on the day when I turned 21! I do not know if the nurse had heard me whisper. She comes to place a thermometer under my arm. I'll never forget that look full of tenderness and love. Her face seemed to be crowned with a sunbeam, 'my guardian angel.' I had not felt such happiness for a very long time, a happiness in my soul and at the same time a new will to fight to live and go home. The nurse looks at the thermometer: 98.6! This is so extraordinary that she wants to check again. Alas, the thermometer slips from her hand

and crashes to the ground, in pieces. She turns pale, picks up the pieces and hurriedly leaves the room.

Waiting to be sent back to a new camp two prisoners did various cleaning tasks, taking care of the dead or taking in new patients. They had begun to spread disinfectants when suddenly the commander burst into the room pulling the nurse by the arm. He yells as loud as ever, overturns everything in his path bearing down on me. He pulls out his revolver, fired into the air and aims the barrel of his gun at my forehead. He spits on me and continues to bark in a mixture of Russian and German: "We'll make soap out of you! Ha! ha! and I will wash my hands with it!" I was resigned that I was going to be killed by this lunatic. I thought of my parents while imploring the protection of the Blessed Virgin and forgiveness of our Lord Jesus Christ. The commander suddenly relented. He apparently had expected to find me in terrified fear and was now baffeled by some kind of serenity that prevented him from firing.

Someones's yelling ends the intensity of the scene. The commander turns around. The doctor and the nurse rush on him, the doctor protesting loudly, chases him out of the room and he retreats waving his arms and swearing. Such a crisis for a thermometer, for that is what it was. The nurse had to report the loss of the thermometer and that's what triggered the fury of the commander. But this time he really went too far. Olga has long suffered under the delusions of this drunkard. She is determined to make a report to his superiors to get him replaced especially now that a delegation of the Red Cross is expected.

In fact, the same day that bully was fired. His replacement almost never left his office where the meetings were held with the doctor and nurses.

This amazing 9th of December 1945 ended with a good soup with white bread for my 21st birthday! I fell asleep exhausted, my soul at peace.

*

Then followed a long road to full recovery. I was still sinking into phases of semi-consciousness. The smile of the nurse stayed with me when I walked through these periods of darkness. Gradually, the contours of my environment became clearer to me as I started to come out of limbo. And what do I see? Men, all very sick without proper care, the nurse and the doctor doing the impossible to give them relief with the help of semi-healed prisoners. The hospital routine was simple: in the morning removing dead and cleaning the beds to receive new patients.

To my right, a patient had replaced the previous one who died during the night. This newcomer was skeletal in particularly bad shape. Yet, in his eyes I saw a glimmer of hope and a call for help. I watched the nurse who despite the man's cadaverous appearance, messy and smelly as he was, offered a divine smile to this human wreck. She seemed to me like an angel incarnate in this hell of misery and disgusting things. Her name was Katarina

- Katarina, I think we can save this guy on the other bed. He must be made to eat something.

- I'm taking care of it.

Katarina first prepared him a drink and an hour later she came back with a thick soup that I gave him, spoon by spoon, which he swallowed with a lot of effort. It exhausted me and I had to lie down again.

With Katarina's care I came to live again. On the eighth day of my 'resurrection' I could take my first steps in my room. Imperceptibly my bed neighbor also started to recover. I wanted to get to know him better. A first attempt at a conversation failed, he was not ready. But I still could see in his eyes that glimmer of hope that had struck me the first time I saw him. I made the sign of the cross on his forehead, saying: "Keep your faith in God and you will survive." One morning, after the soup, I made another attempt at a dialogue. This time he seemed willing to talk:

"I was born in January 1919 in a village in Mecklenburg. My parents had a very large farm, a lot of land and woods 20 miles from Schwerin. I never worked on the farm. At 18 I went to the University of Greifswald to study engineering. At 22, I got my degree and I voluntered in a tank unit. When I think about this... We were so eager to go to war! Of course, no 'final victory' for us! In 1943, at Minsk, my tank division fought very hard and I was promoted to lieutenant. I commanded a Tiger tank. My tank was hit by a T-34 and I owe my life to the courage of an NCO who pulled me out of the tank as it burst in flames. I was hurt and they transported me to a field hospital. After first aid a Red Cross truck took me 60 miles behind the front.

Two months later I was back on my feet for a three week furlough. That was in November 1943. I went to my parents and I took the opportunity to visit Berlin, that is to say what was left after the bombing. Here in Mecklenburg we were still spared. I had made a request to celebrate Christmas with my family, especially since my parents had already lost one son. My request was denied and I had to go back to the front. In December 1943 I joined a reserve battalion in a small town in Pomerania. Five days later I received my marching orders to the headquarters of the Army Centre Corps. In 1944 we fought while retreating. Next to our Tiger division was the tank division "Charlemagne" with French vounteers. They were fearless fighters. The Russians were scared of them. But in late 1944 we were encircled by the Red Army. The Charlemagne division was cut down but continued to fight. Then our life as prisoners began. At first we were rebuilding railway tracks, bridges, roads and everything that needed repair.

"In mid-March we were crammed into cattle cars towards Moscow and were herded into a transit camp on the outskirts of Moscow. We did not know what we were doing there. The last few weeks they starved us with almost nothing to eat, just enough to stay alive. But then, about April 15, we were served a hearty soup with vegetables and potatoes, a very rich soup, as much as we wanted. Inevitably, we overdid it, gulping down two, three portions, not suspecting anything, just taking one more mouthful. And then suddenly: Dawai, dawai, everyone in trucks towards the center of Moscow. Without time to rest we were pushed off the trucks and herded into rows of ten to trudge along a wide venue lined with bleachers on each side filled with crowds of Russians to see us pass. Obviously, after weeks of dry bread and water all this rich soup began to take effect, perhaps they had even added a laxative. In short, shit started to flow down our legs. Those behind us slid and floundered in a sea of shit. The crowd bellowed in unison "Nix cultura! Nix cultura!" When we got to the first Moscow camp we saw a newspaper photo of this fucking parade with the titles: "The Nazis in Moscow!" or "The glorious German army!" The truth is that ever since that memorable day that I can't get rid of this wretched diarrhea. I remember that you made a sign of the cross on my forehead. You are a believer. My family and me never were. There was a Protestant church in our village but we never set foot in it. Never. Anyway, in 1934 the pastor had left and the church closed."

This long talk had exhausted us. We both fell asleep.

*

As I regained strength I could make myself useful and started to assist the nurse. The most afflicted men could not stand upright and we had to carry them to the bucket and support them while they were trying with great difficulty to void. They could not wash or feed themselves or take their medication. Ultimately, I got the official assignment as 'caregiver', but what horrible conditions! You had to have a strong stomach and a great love of your fellow men to face an environment where death, filth, stench and suffering reigned supreme! At least my taking on these tasks were recognized not only by the nurse but also by the doctor. They complimented me on my dedication to my fellow men.

Katarina told me that the reason she had hired me was mainly to avoid that I would be forced too early to go to another camp. I thanked her. She had tears in her eyes while a feeling of intense happiness came over me. This nurse was truly a godsend!

My work with the sick gave me access to medical facilities in the 'hospital', that is to say access to ... nothing. But it was the opportunity to walk through the halls and to try to track down former comrades of the camp 367. Thus I found Edmond Lorrain and another comrade of our group. Edmond was in agony. I do not think he recognized me. With another friend, we review the names of such and such. Many were dead. Some, barely recovered, already left for another camp. He should leave the hospital soon, probably before Christmas. Sure, he would have preferred to stay here where it was at least warm. Then we returned to Edmond. Some days he was a little better but then had suddenly relapses. I went to his bed to try to talk to him. No answer. His body was burning with fever, he was panting with endless coughing. Edmond, my French friend, my revolutionary, always ready to help others, you will leave your body here in this hostile land and you will join the hundreds of thousands of anonymous missing, nobody to let your family know about your suffering, nobody has your address, no one can keep any paper, everything was confiscated, no trace, nothing. And I thought of the cross and the medal of the Blessed Virgin that I once had in my pocket. They all had disappeared, probably between the camp and the arrival to the hospital, but I had found my wallet in my clothes.

I took Edmonds hands and prayed for him as I had done so many times for other soldiers: "Our Father who art in heaven, hallowed be thy name, thy kingdom come thy will be done, on earth as in heaven. Lord our God, after these terrible events and all his suffering, grant Edmond forgiveness for his sins and give him eternal peace." And by making the sign of the cross on his forehead, I said "Amen."

Edmond was no longer breathing.

On returning to our room, my bed neighbor called me:

- What do you have to do to become a believer like you?

- It is very simple. You have to ask, that is to say, pray to God to forgive your sins and protect you now and throughout your life.

I taught him the 'Our Father' and told him to always start his prayer with the sign of the cross, saying, "In the name of the Father, the Son and the Holy Spirit." His name was Heinrich and he wished he could soon become a 'caregiver', too. I thanked him with a smile.

*

Katarina had great hopes that the 'probable' visit of a delegation of the International Red Cross would improve conditions in the hospital. Meanwhile, we continued in our routine to take the dead from their beds in the morning and make the beds ready for the new patients an hour later!

Shortly before Christmas, a particular patient had intrigued me. Despite his physical decay neither his eyes nor his general countenance had lost their somewhat remote dignity. He had not succumbed to his suffering nor plunged into confusion. I felt that his strength must be rooted in a deep humanity. I thought him to be in his 60's and I was surprised that he had been able to fight the disease for so long.

I made the first move and started a conversation. His perfectly controlled German betrayed some superior education. His name was Ludovic Esterhazy. He told me that he was assigned to the reconstruction of administrative buildings of a steel complex and despite all his precautions he had caught this terrible dysentery. He thought would survive based on his medical knowledge and the dedication by the nurse. He believed that the worst was behind him.

- Are you a doctor?

"Yes, I am a doctor and I have, or had, a private clinic in Budapest. I am 43, with a wife and three children. After the entry of the Red Army in Budapest my clinic was requisitioned. With my team we had to work for the army under the Russian military doctors. My car and my apartment in Budapest had been requisitioned by the Soviets. I had sent my family to our country house, about twenty miles from the capital. I took the train every morning to the clinic. On May 12, I was on the platform of our small suburban station as usual. A cattle car train full of prisoners bound for Russia stopped in front of us. We had already seen trains like that pass but none of us civilians were ever arrested. This time soldiers descended from the train guns in hand screaming and grabbing a dozen of us at random forcing us into two of the cattle cars. That is how I became a 'prisoner of war'! Since that day my family has had no news of me and I do not know what became of them. Of course,when I arrived at the camp I made several complaints but the reaction of the political commissar made me quickly understand that it was better to shut up. Anyway, they took all my papers and my clothes. And now, with my rotten old Red Army uniform I am indeed considered a prisoner of war! The nurse told me that a delegation from the Red Cross may be coming and that gives me some hpe that I can set things straight again."

So the rumor was true. There were many prisoners of war, despite themselves, who had been randomly picked up by the Red Army and sent to Russia. How many of them had disappeared en route dying of hunger or exhaustion? And how many women were raped and killed by gangs of wild marouders or even by fighters from the front lines? My Hungarian doctor knew that as well as I. He was very worried about his family.

At the first opportunity, I spoke to Katarina about him to convince her he would make a valuable nurse in this hospital. No answer. But in the days that followed somehow his food rations had increased.

*

On the 23rd of December Katarina asked me to follow her. Among a batch of new patients I found Karl Schmidt, the man from the Fulda area. I had met him with another prisoner, Otto Fischer of Neuhof/Fulda, on the road from Prague to Brno. After that we had lost touch.

What a pity to find poor Karl severely burnt all over his body! He, a strapping six footer, 30 years old, had become a human wreck. I immediately asked Katarina permission to take him with us. She could not see why not.

The next day, helped by my Hungarian doctor, we installed Karl in our room and placed his bed in a corner near mine. Katarina had obviously noticed that I gave special attention to this patient though he had not yet recognized me. She had prepared a sweet porridge for him to make him perk up. I sat Karl up, took him into my arms and fed him like a baby. After that he fell into a deep sleep as if dead. The doctor, Katarina and Ludovic quickly answered my unspoken question: "It would be a miracle if he survives the night!" They were unanimous.

I asked Olga permission to organize a Christmas party for Karl and the other patients, in fact, for everyone. With a simple nod accompanied by a shrug of her shoulders she indicates that she does not object. I said to myself that maybe she will give permission to all her staff to join us.

Katarina and Ludovic joined in without hesitation. Could we find a Christmas tree and a few things to decorate it and three or four candles? A tree? Katarina did not see how we could possibly get one. There are no trees in the camp and none around the hospital. It could perhaps find a piece of wax to make candles. How to celebrate Christmas without a tree? Taking a look outside, I see a bundle of bare branches about three feet high, some kind of bush, perhaps a thistle or something like that. That's my Christmas tree! I ran and told Katarina. She did not believe this could work but agreed to accompany me to the commander. He was a brave officer who, after listening to the nurse, let me get these skeletal branches.

I put on boots, my military coat, and the commander even lends me his fur hat and a hatchet. It was cold outside, at the very least - 40 F. Trudging through the knee deep snow I get to my 'Christmas tree'. With its dry branches it could have passed for a bunch of barbed wire. Whatever!

I cut carefully and retracing my steps, I saw in the corner against a wall a pile of corpses, naked.

Thanking the commander for his help, I could not help but wonder about the destination of corpses. Simply, every two or three days a truck would pick them up, that's all. He shook his head.

Katarina and I carried my 'tree' into a room which served as refectory for the hospital staff. I began preparations for a party for my friends, at least those who could make it, a Christmas party like at home! The thought filled me with joy, a contagious joy. Nurses, the doctor and even the commander gradually lent a hand. This celebration of Christmas was a first in their hospital and probably the last. Somehow I felt I had changed the mindset of the Russian staff. The indifference, if not hostility, of the doctor and the commander had given place to a sincere interest.

We cobbled together a base to stabilize our 'tree' while a nurse was melting the wax and manufactured four candles which we attached to the more sturdy of the branches. The doctor gave us a piece of red cloth and another green one that we tied into bows for the branches. Finally, I cut a star from a piece of cardboard, colored it yellow and attached it to the top of the 'tree' - our Christmas star!

Without hesitation the commander agreed to distribute the soup earlier than usual. And tonight it would be served with two slices of white bread. I read my own thoughts in the eyes of Katarina: what a change of mood in so little time!

The good news of our preparations spread fast. Two orderlies from the rooms on the ground floor asked if they could attend our Christmas party. After talking to Katarina I of course agreed: "And any of your patients who can walk are also welcome!"

We should not forget our own patients. Ludovic, Heinrich and my neighbor returned with Karl. He vaguely regained consciousness. He recognized me. I took the opportunity to tell him about the story of Christmas, of the birth of Christ, but soon enough I realized that he was no longer listening to me. In his state, the same state as I had known three weeks earlier, the feelings of the heart and mind do not exist. Karl had reached and exceeded the unbearable. The point of no return was inscribed on his face and in his body.

Poor Karl! You never will know freedom! Your life ends miserably, behind barbed wire. Nobody will ever put flowers on your grave because you will not have one. But I promise you, if God willing, I will see your parents again and I will tell them about you, your courage in the face of death. All I could do was to surround his last moments with a little warmth and love.

At 6pm, a pleasant surprise: they had added a portion of "kasha", a kind of semolina puree to our soup. Many of the sick, exhausted after a few bites, could not finish their ration. Our meal was becoming a real feast for those with an appetite for both.

I wanted Karl to swallow some of the sweet porridge that the nurse had prepared. Nothing doing. He was still alive but totally unresponsive.

After the meal I moved my bed to the side to create a little space for my 'Christmas tree', standing on a small table taken from the refectory. A nurse in her white coat put it on a placemat. While we were doing this I watched the reaction of the orderlies from the corner of my eyes. The patients from the other floors joined us with their caregivers. Some of these were on the road to recovery, others, their eyes shining with fever, looked at my tree with looks of hope and sadness.

The commander himself was there alongside the doctor and two nurses. Katarina encouraged me with her eyes as if saying "Go ahead, tell them! It is time!"

My attention was focused on the star, the star that guided the Magi to the Divine child. I felt a transformation take place in me expanding my heart and my soul. Imperceptibly a joy of emotion came over me. Yes, the most beautiful gift of God, this joy in its purest form, this inalienable joy made possible an incredible inner turmoil: I had a light heart! All the misery was transfigured. This thistle twig shriveled by the winter? A beautiful tree. This cardboard star? Light, nothing but light!

A silence fell around me. Then I spoke of our Christian Christmas, the joy of this celebration of the birth of Christ, our Savior come to earth to save us from our sins, that we love one another as brothers .

"Peace on earth for all of good will".

And I talked about our families who were without news from us for so long, but now for sure, thinking of us more than any other day and praying for us as we were praying for them. I recited the 'Our Father'. Around me, one by one, voices joined me praying fervently, some barely audible but full of hope, uniting those dying with those convalescents. "Forgive us our trespasses as we forgive those who trespass against us. And lead us not into temptation but deliver us from evil. Amen."

The prayer ended, and in the silence that followed I wanted to light the tree. The commander had thought about it, he strikes a match and a little flame rises humbly from our four candles. I immediately start singing the most famous carol of all: "Stille Nacht, heilige Nacht ... Silent night, holy night ..." Ludovic the Hungarian, nurses, patients, those who were on the ground floor, all fall in singing with in unison to announce the birth of Christ our Savior. Then there are other songs culminating in the "Gloria" at the end of which I can not restrain my tears of joy. Why would I repressed them? Leaving my tears to flow it felt as if I freed myself from the terrible burden that threatened to destroy in me all human feeling.

The eyes of the audience also shone. Ludovic, Katarina, the other nurses and many patients still had the ability to cry and with it came hope. I approached Karl. A sort of smile seemed frozen on his face. When I took his hands I realized he was no longer of this world. And always that strange smile that was aimed more at us but went far, far away. Perhaps we had made him more human in his last moments? God rest his soul!

"Your friend is dead. You knew him a long time?" I nodded, unable to say more to Katarina. She told me that the doctor wanted to talk to me and Ludovic. She left before the end of the celebration as did the commander. Ludovic was as surprised as me: no prisoner had ever crossed the threshold of Olga's office.

*

"Come in!"

Olga was sitting behind here desk and invited us to sit down in front of her.

First, nothing happens. She hesitates for quite a while. Then suddenly something changes. The ice is broken. Our celebration has revived memories in her of Orthodox Christmas celebrations that are now banned in the Soviet Union. Now her childhood, her youth and her former life come up to the surface. She speaks freely as if broken out of a shell in which she had been locked up for years trying to shield herself of all human feeling. Here she remembers her youth in Moscow, her years of college, meeting her future husband, their happy years together, both doctors, he a celebrated surgeon, she a most sought after women doctor. In 1925, she gave birth to twins, filling the couple with unbounded joy. But staring in 1939 with the German-Soviet pact their happiness gradually erodes. The professional reputation of Olga's husband continues to rise but he is suddenly arrested, accused of plotting against the Soviet Union. Ten years of gulag, never returned. A conspiracy? The usual pretext for the Stalinist purges, especially in the medical profession. The truth is that he was a Jew, even if he does not practice his religion. For the Soviets in power, he is not Russian, he is a potential traitor that must be eliminated.

Olga wanted to talk and we all let her talk without interruption, without question. We were the audience that she had chosen to lay down the heavy burden of her personal history that she is prohibited to share. We measure the immense trust she must have in our integrity not ever to betray her. Yes, definitely, this Christmas celebration in 1945 was a deliverance for all, a true healing of the soul.

*

CHAPTER 11

Back to the Mines!

I was still in the hospital but what a change! Olga broke into a big smile as soon as she saw me in the morning. The captain even bothered to greet us, both Ludovic and me. Katarina still radiated goodness and sweetness. Olga had told Ludovic that the visit of the Red Cross delegation was scheduled for mid-January.

Heinrich had been declared cured and had left the hospital. Ludovic and I had been recruited as new 'caregivers'. Even without drugs we became 'good Samaritans' and became experienced to 'cure by example', convinced that love for others can sometimes do wonders.

On December 31, a large number of new patients were admitted. They were in a mess. Olga, Katarina and two nurses first sorted them. Those who were at their worst would remain on the ground floor. We installed the others on the first and second floor where we spread 'mattresses' on the floor. The whole day was spent with these chores. We were so tired that we threw ourselves on our beds without even eating, falling asleep instantly, frequently to be awakened by the screams of the newcomers. We rushed to comfort them but we knew that some of them would not see the sun rise.

Indeed, at dawn the toll was heavy: eight prisoners had died. We laid them near the exit and called the gravedigger detachment to take the bodies. Katarina administered her sweet broth to those who could not swallow anything else. Even the liquid was hard to ingest for many of them. They were so weak that they could not move by themselves and as hard as we tried to nourish them to gain strength they were unable to get to the toilet so that we constantly had to replace their soiled mattresses. Serving soup to those who kept a bit of mobility seemed like a breeze in comparison. We, ourselves, could not eat our rations until all these tasks had been completed. Katarina told Olga about our heroic efforts and she thanked us warmly, wishing us a Happy 1946 and especially a good recovery for an early release from this hellish place.

The new year began. Could we wish for anything better than that it would bring us freedom and the happiness of seeing our families? Ludovic and I were reminiscing:

- With the help of God I will be back home in a few months. Last time I celebrated the New Year was with my friends in Potsdam where we just had become lieutenants. I even got to call my family. A few days after we joined the front in Silesia. And you probably celebrated the New Year with your family?

- Yes, we were in our apartment in Budapest with some friends but we were not really in a partying mood because we knew that the Red Army was advancing rapidly. In Budapest the Communist Party members were secretely preparing an uprising to welcome the Russians, but not secretly enough, because the Hungarian intelligence services with the help of the Germans stopped them and shot all of them. At least that is what was said afterwards.

Our daily work continued. In mid-January, the Red Cross delegation arrived at the hospital for its inspection. They stopped in our room. We were busy feeding the sick. They watched us a

144

few moments and, having sniffed the stench in the room they quickly left for the refectory, the largest room in the hospital.

Ludovic was received by the delegation. He was asked to provide all his information, including on his first camp, where his papers were confiscated. The head of the delegation promised he would be released as soon as possible and that he would return to Hungary with other compatriots already gathered in a camp not far from here.

As soon as the delegation had left Katarina told me that the hospital would soon receive their first supply of medications, new thermometers and mattresses and all prisoners were to receive a Red Cross postcard to write to their families. We were elated. At least we could now tell our family that we were still alive!

*

Olga and Katarina kept me as a caregiver as they long as they could but eventually their cunning would reached its limits. They could no longer hide my recovery. In late January it would be over and I would have to go. The hospital commander asked me if I had a preference for a camp. Of course!

- I'd like to see my friends who are in a camp north of Donbass. The director of the mining complex is called Boris.

- I'll find out, I will assign you there as soon as I have located the camp. But I must fill a complete truck with other healed prisoners.

Two days later, the commander called me: "I found your former camp, it is camp 220, about 20 miles from here. Tomorrow morning I'll get a truck. You will leave with twenty other prisoners and two military guards."

After thanking him I went to see Katarina and Olga. They already knew. We had dinner together in Olga's office. The atmosphere was morose. I spoke to the two women:

- Olga, Christmas has transformed all of us. Today you are to me a woman who has rediscovered that you have the capacity to love. You became like a mother to me. And you, Katarina, my guardian angel, you were my sunshine, a gift from heaven. I will never forget you.

The next morning we were served a good soup and white bread. Before boarding the truck, Olga, Katarina and the commander came to me to say goodbye. Olga and Katarina kissed me on the mouth - intensely - they had tears in their eyes. "We will never forget you." The commander shook my hand and in true Russian fashion wished me a 'good winter'.

Witnessing these warm farewells the other prisoners were perplexed, not daring to ask for more. I did not feel like talking. Let's hope that our destination will be a good one! I was sure that I had made the right choice by asking for this camp, but how could I know that nothing had changed there? In this absurd Soviet system policies kept changing and people were often moved around according to incomprehensible criteria. One could expect anything. Then my thoughts wandered. I thought that the Russians or Ukrainians had retained a deep attachment to religion after all. They did not have the right to express it openly but in small groups they could do it with pride provided that they were sure that nobody was around to denounce them. In this sense Christmas 1945 was a revelation to me.

*

The camp was the one I had left because of my dysentery but the commander had changed. His replacement greeted us. Since I was the only one who had been there before I introduced myself. He had heard about me:

- I will inform the Director. Boris often asked about you. But as you know it's nearly impossible to get to see him.

- And the former commander?

- He made too many mistakes, especially with the drinking water. Boris brought in the health service. From there on he was no longer effective and he was fired. Upon my arrival, I gave the order to boil the kitchen water to make it drinkable. Since then no more problems. In addition, as the mining complex produces a lot of coal beyond the 'norm' our camp earned several benefits, like much better food. Let's call Boris.

Boris was delighted to hear from me and to learn that I had returned to the camp: "Your men are extraordinary. Week after week we keep producing a lot of coal. We'll talk tomorrow."

The commander decided to put me in my old barracks so that I could be with my old team. The prisoner delegate had already distributed the other newcomers. He was also glad to see me. Still the same Pole from Krakow. He was no longer a novice. He had lived through the dysentery epidemic and the change of direction of the camp. Were there other comrades that were sick?

- Yes, in your hut there were six and several others elsewhere, altogether forty prisoners but thanks to our director's intervention, the former commander was replaced. Two water containers were contaminated. The new containers are fine.

- Who was in charge of the group during my absence?

- No one. Everyone was waiting for your return.

- So I take my old place.

- It's almost noon, I'll look for a good soup and bread or rather, I'll ask the captain if he will lunch with us in his office.

The commander was waiting for me:

- You know you've left the impression in the entire complex of someone exceptional! Basically, I do not really know why. I'm not aware what's special about you but perhaps you can enlighten me?

- Major, are you Ukrainian?

- Yes.

- Are you a believer?

- I am told you are.

- Who told you?

- Boris, he is Ukrainian, like me.

I noticed he had evaded the question about his religious faith. I learned that he was 32, a major. He had been in the battle of Leningrad from beginning to end. He spoke of this very tough battle and their heroic resistance. I told him about my stay at the hospital and Olga and her two sons who died in Leningrad. A new connecting of human beings was established.

The prisoner delegate arrived at my sickbed with my meager soup and one single slice of black bread.

- By the way, what is your name? I asked him.

- My name is Karel, a very common name in the Krakow region. Poland is catholic and especially our region. Lieutenant, I know that you, too, are catholic and deeply religious. Your comrades told me everything and they are proud to be believers with you. And they told me of your victory over the former commissar, Friedrich's funeral and the prayer meeting with the entire camp.

The commander listened to Karel's story with great interest, but without comment. Then he turned to me:

- I'd like to talk to you one day. But I think your friends will be here soon and you will have many things to tell them.

Karel accompanied me back to my hut.

First surprise: the hut was heated.

- Yes, in principle there is always a guy who is sick who has to light the stove before the teams return from work. But as there are no sick ones here I asked the guy next door to take care of it because it's already cold out there!

Now I was alone in the hut, alone with my thoughts, and with them comes introspection. Ever since I was in captivity, the evidence had only increased that the only force that kept the men alive was through faith in God. But how many of us knew how to pray? How many had forgotten? Should I start to work like some kind of 'missionary'? No, I was not a priest, that was not part of my life path. And yet, from camp to camp, I had crossed so many unhappy men, mostly German but also from other European countries. I could measure the extent of the devastation in their minds caused by the inhuman conditions of our captivity. Much of it was the aftermath of the wretched Nazi ideology. All those who were not protected by a solid religious education had succumbed to the cult of Nazi 'Providence' that today was no help for them.

Our captivity had disoriented them, deprived them of inner strength. They were lost in this new environment, physically exhausted and mentally crushed. To them I had become a pillar of strength that they could lean on, a man, moreover an officer, who inspired confidence because he was a believer. Every time I took a look at myself the figure of my father would come up with his words: "By loving your neighbor and helping the weak, God will love you". He also used to tell me that my upbringing in our catholic family will sustain me throughout my life. No, I was not a priest but by giving my comrades new hope through prayer I could save many lives.

I was pulled from my meditation by a commotion coming from outside. What a great reunion! Everyone was talking at once: "Lieutenant! Lieutenant! What a joy to see you! We were certain that you would come back! It's been so long, more than two months, but we never lost hope." The happiness and joy that I read in their eyes were cheering me up and I gave thanks to God for allowing me to be back. There is not a more intense emotion than the joy of a reunion.

- And the other comrades who had dysentery?

- You were the first to come down with it. The others the very next day.

- And our comrades from Stalingrad?

- They were with them. We have had no news from them since.

The commander and Karel were watching from a distance. I made them a sign to share in this reunion. What about the mine?

"All is well" said Wilhelm. "Boris is looking forward to meeting with you. Besides, he has let us out early to welcome you. But tell us about yourself, what has your life been like?"

Better to go into the hut where it was warm. The commander and Karel followed us there. Once again, I told my adventures in detail. A long silence greeted the end of my story. Karel then took the floor to say that I really must have been protected by Heaven.

- How about getting something to eat?

The commander invited me to dinner the next evening.

To the soup kitchen! I suggested we would again take up our good marching habits. Everyone in rows of four and forward march! The head of the canteen was flabbergasted seeing us arrive so orderly in a neat column with my military salute. He did not know what to make of it. How would these men accept my way of keeping up military discipline? My men had no trouble seeing the immediate benefit: the chef filled our tin cans to the brim and gave us two slices of white bread.

Inside we took our coats off and turned them into cushions for the chairs. Katharina had given me a clean coat matching the fur cap from the hospital commander, all in very good condition. "Like a true Russian lieutenant!" exclaimed Bernard. "Yes, but he's missing the shoulder stripes! Perhaps they will give him those as a next thing!" With much laughter the happiness of the reunion continued. They egged me on with their friendly heckling. So many emotions and also so much fatigue.

- My dear friends, it is time to go to bed and before we fall asleep everyone should think about a little prayer. Let's thank the Lord for allowing us to be together again.

*

After forming our regular column and saluting the commander the next day, we left for the mine,. He, too, was surprised about our military bearing. We walked briskly through the snow and ice and it is quite cold.

Boris greeted me warmly with immediate congratulations for my team's excellent work.

- Ever since they dealt with the pump motors and the motor for the elevator and lifts everything works perfectly, and we produce coal at a rate exceeding all standards!

- Who works in the mines?

- Your comrades. They gave us a good production system and the recovery of coal has been facilitated by new wagons. In addition, I have built a heated hut for their lunch time. And at the end of the day everyone can take a hot shower.

- And the water is clean?

- Oh yes, and always will be.

I thought about all this. Doing productive work, having a purpose, made their hard life as prisoners somewhat more tolerable, especially now that they're being treated a lot better. At the same time they had earned the repect of their Russian captors. A good thing for all.

While I was pondering about our prisoner life Boris phoned someone and I could make out my name in the middle of his Russian. Five men arrived shortly after, four mine directors and a political commissar. Boris suggested we shared tea:

- Our friend will tell us an incredible but true story. The camp commander called me this morning to tell me about it.

Then Boris and I were alone again.

- Boris, what will you want me to work on?

- Aloys, for now you will be my guest, nothing else. I have a debt of gratitude to you. Nothing prevents you to go for a ride to the mine to see your specialists, but first we eat soup together in my office. In the evening you can take a shower before your comrades come back from the mine.

Boris had called me by my first name.

It was noon. The translator came to set the table: two real earthware soup plates, two spoons and two glasses! It seemed I had not seen this for decades and my astonishment was very visible:

- Ah yes ! You do not believe it! There's been a change here in the last two months! As my mining complex produces far beyond the standards they treat me with kid gloves and it is you and your team that has made this possible.

Since it was not really urgent for me to return to work right now we stayed together after the meal. Curiosity made me ask Boris about his political views. I knew this could be risky.

151

- Boris, my friend, I believe that Stalin did not like the Ukrainians. He has millions of deaths on his conscience except, of course, he has no conscience. No one can resist this man. Do you think he will remain number one for long? Do not hurry, Boris, think!

- I trust you to hear this, and I will tell you what we Ukrainians really think. Stalin has more enemies than friends. And he will not die a natural death. When? Impossible to say. I hope as soon as possible.

- I think like you.

I got up to shake his hand. Since the time I was around camp commanders, the managers and directors of mines and even the hospital staff I had learned a lot about the Soviet Union, about their views of Stalin, about life before and after the war and communist revolution. I had no trouble agreeing with Boris.

We returned from the mine in the evening again in tight formation. Passing the commander I give him my military salute. He acknowledges with a broad smile saying "See you soon again!"

Back at camp the commander serves the soup in the same earthware dish as Boris.

- Yesterday Boris told me that you have become something like friends. With your work and the dedication of your team to do such good work you have shown us that here there are neither victors nor vanquished. This is remarkable and I have never seen such a good attitude. I have good news for all of you. The Red Cross told me that in two weeks you will receive the first postcard for your families. I will tell you as soon as I have them. For now, no need to tell your friends.

*

The next two weeks passed like a dream. Boris worked close with me making a point of including me in his decision making. It looked like he was afraid of losing me. My team and other camp mates had only one idea: let's hope it will last! We were in late

February and spring was in the air. Sunny days had given way to the winter cold in the Donbass.

In early March it got even warmer. We no longer had to heat our hut. The commander called me to his office. I see immediately the postcards with the red cross.

- This is probably one of the happiest days for a prisoner of war. You will be able to give your families some news from you.

It was a double postcard: the first part was for us to fill out, the second part for our family's response. The text was printed in French and Russian.

- Eat with your teammates and then I want to see the leaders of each hut to explain how to fill out the first part.

The announcement of this good news first surprised everyone and then a round of applause broke out. Happiness shone in the eyes of all.

After the soup the barracks leaders assembled at the commander's office. He gave gave each his card and a pen to write our first message. The address of my parents was already typed on it. The commander then dictated what we had to write: "Dear Family or relative or friend, happy to give you my first news. I'm fine and I hope that soon we will be reunited. I think of you with all my heart." Signature and name.

- Commander, is that all?

- Yes, sorry, that's all. This is all you are allowed to say, otherwise the censors will destroy your card. As you can see on back of the response card is your name, the address of the Red Cross in Moscow and then below, the number of your mailbox is already typed in. Your parents will only have to complete the front. Your family's reply card will follow you wherever you will be since your camp or hospital record always follows you.

Despite all their faults we had to concede that the Soviets had a formidable sense of organization. This was simply a part of their system. Bureaucracy has always been a hobby of the communist parties.

Each barracks leader received their teammates cards for the prisoners to fill out according to the instruction from the commander. The next morning we gave the cards to the delegate who assured us that they would leave the same day.

In late March we received orders to go to a new camp, 1500 of us. My barracks team was leaving together. We were happy we could stay together but we left for the unknown and were leaving a camp where we had found a tolerable life.

The morning of departure, we received a double portion of soup and six slices of bread. We boarded a freight train, forty people per car. Compared to previous trips we were travelling in great comfort.

*

CHAPTER 12

A Prisoner's Life can be Full of Surprises

We left camp 220 around noon. The next day, after a journey of 300 miles, they gave us water and a slice of black bread and told us to get off the train. After two hours of walking we arrived at a huge construction site with decent looking camp barracks designed to house a hundred prisoners. There was a lot of barbed wire and mountains of lumber. The camp commander and the prisoner delegate showed us our barracks. As always I was named the barrack leader responsible for 99 prisoners. Once again the delegate was a Polish prisoner who had arrived with the first convoy four weeks earlier. His name was Ladislav. He asked the officers to step forward and told them: "We have already built thirty-two new barracks working from 6am to 8pm. There remain eight more to build. This will be your job starting tomorrow. Latrines are at either end of the camp, right and left. There are signs. We have already finished work around the central square where the kitchens are located. Those who have just arrived are going to build the last barracks for 800 men who in the meanwhile will sleep in tents near the entrance."

Luckily, my friends and I were able to settle in the same barrack, number 4.

We worked hard for two weeks to complete the camp. Our rations were meager but we have had others that were a lot less. What would be in store for us afterwards?

The delegate is happy to see me.

- You know, sir, that you are a real hero. Your comrades told me everything. It's incredible. I repeated all this to the commander and he invites you tonight for soup.

- What day is it today ?

- It's April 15 and it is precisely 5:30 (by what mystery did he still have a watch?).

- Thank you.

Back at the barracks my comrades assaulted me with questions: "Oh, sir, did you see the prisoner delegate? He happened by here and he was rather curious. He wanted information about you and whether we had been together for long. So we told him that we worked together for quite a while already. That surprised him and he left."

What about them? I could see a certain pride in their eyes, but I felt that they had become a little too presumptuous:

- Comrades, you do not know the delegate, much less the commander. We are new here. Let's not jump to conclusions, remain cautious. True, we shared a lot of unique situations but for the moment let us keep them for ourselves. I always try to watch over you but I repeat: be cautious. The commander invited me for soup tonight but I do not know what's up. I do not even know if the delegate will be there. I'll tell you all about it later.

The delegate came to pick me up. When he introduced me to the commander I saluted him and thanked him for meeting with me.

The commander told me about the history of the camp from its beginnings.

"When we came here there was nothing, nothing. We arrived with a very dynamic political commissar who directs the work of this great project and with several engineers and a truck with twenty prisoners. The Commissar said it would be a camp for 4000 prisoners and as a first thing we had to lay out the required space. The prisoners and two guards would sleep in a tent while they installed the posts for the barbed wire fence. Two more trucks arrived the next day with equipment and building materials. I had to supervise the work with the engineers. Other prisoners come in as reinforcements when needed. And off we went! Today our camp is almost finished. Soon we will be ready for the big project for which this camp is being built."

- What big project are you talking about?

- The final project is the construction of an Italian Fiat car factory to be named after the leader of the Italian Communist Party, Togliatti," he said as he was reading from a paper: "Togliattigrad"!

- Commander, I believe you are former military?

- Yes, I'm a Lieutenant Colonel, I'm 39 years old. I did all the Great Patriotic War campaigns up to early 1945. I was wounded twice and for me the war ended just before the entrance into Berlin because I was pretty badly hurt. I was first treated at a hospital in Gdansk where the majority of doctors and nurses were German, all very competent. They did an outstanding job. Without them, I would have lost my leg. Since then, my opinion of the Germans has changed a lot. I find them good people but they had chosen a very bad leaders, like us! I tell you the truth, because I know that you are a believer,' so I trust you.

- How do you know ?

- From the prisoner delegate. He is Polish and a believer, too. The rest he learned from your comrades. You know that for me, who controls this camp, the presence of someone like you is very important. I looked at your file and I saw the comments. By the way, can you show me your wallet?

- Yes, but who told you about it?

- Your last commander slipped a note in the file.

So I showed him my wallet. He looked at it carefully:

- The dead soldiers, were they family?

- They were my cousins and one was a very close friend.
- Your parents were very religious. That was risky under Hitler.
I nodded.

The delegate returned with three servings of soup and three slices of black bread. The commander ate with us even though he was a very senior officer. The evening was very instructive. I learned many details that would surely be helpful for me in the coming months. The commander spoke excellent German. The delegate was of the same caliber.

- Commander, what's the next weeks program?
- You will build a four mile road that leads to an empty plain, just like here before. After that I do not know. The commissar is the one who knows, he is the one who directs the work. I take care of the camp. In the coming days we will begin to install showers. It will get increasingly hot and you will be glad to be able to wash every evening.

When I returned to my comrades no one dared to ask questions. I reassured them that both the commander and the deputy had made a good impression on me. "But it's a start and I will tell you more as we go."

*

We worked like crazy until mid-May to complete the road. The commissar, still quite young, met often with us and told us that we had exceeded the 'norms' and as a result we were entitled to better food.

- I've done this for you already for the last two weeks.
- I noticed, Comrade Commissar. Excellent! The commander had told me. Thank you in the name of all my comrades.

In early May, we received new Red Cross post cards and everyone was able to give some news to their families, always as dictated by the commander but I slipped a few more words in to say that I had not yet received a response.

The weather was was very nice. We changed to Red Army summer clothes.

In late May the road was finished, a road worthy of the name after a steamroller had made a few passes. The plain stretched before us as far as the eye could see, empty, without even a shrub. I seemed to be able to distinguish a village in the distance. Before returning to the camp, the commissar waved to me. I walked over to him with some suspicion because, like a black SS uniform during the reign of the Nazis a Soviet commissar held all the power:

- I know all about you, all your past and also that you are a believer. So I can trust you. I will need you soon. You will be very useful to me. Do not tell anyone, neither the commander nor your comrades. Oh, one more thing. Tomorrow you will stay at the camp and then you will be transported by truck to save time.

My comrades were curious: "What did the commissar want?"

"He told me to tell you he was very impressed with your work and asked me to thank you. And tomorrow we will stay at the camp and after that we will be moved in trucks not to waste time to get to our work."

Until then we left on foot, as usual. The commander was not there to greet us. The barrack leaders had to report to his office after the shower.

There he began by thanking us for our good work. Through our efforts, the food is much improved and tomorrow we will rest. The delegate spoke: "And now the good news! Mail has arrived for some of you from your families. I sorted it by barracks. Many of your comrades will certainly disappointed because they have no response yet. This applies especially for regions like Silesia, Pomerania and East Prussia that Germany has lost. Those comrades whose families are now in the areas occupied by the Red Army, the Americans, the British or the French should come to me tomorrow morning after the soup. I am at their disposal to help them. We still have some cards for them."

The first card from my parents! For them, it was joy to see that I was alive. My mother said this in her message. Yes, I was still living at the moment and perhaps the worst was perhaps behind us, but who knows! I distributed the response cards. Big smiles lighting up the faces of those who had this first word from their family. Big disappointment for others. To reassure them I repeated Ladislav's words: "He still has Red Cross cards and he will give you all the information to get in touch with your loved ones. And now, all form ranks to go for the soup!"

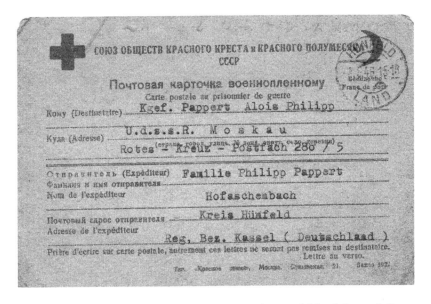

We found it to be excellent with two slices of black bread. It was a fine evening. My men were still concerned about the upcoming program and I had to reassure them again and again.

*

As announced, twenty trucks took us to the road. Each of them carried thirty prisoners, unguarded. Ten minutes later we arrived at our work site. The commissar was already there, flanked by four men. He motioned me to join him. The others were watching from a distance. He presented the four men, all engineers, the planning authorities of the future camp. When he asked me if I had a specialist in my team, I called Wilhelm. One of the engineers spoke German, the others understood some. Perfect.

Arm in arm the commissar walked with me to a jeep bringing me up to date about his engineers and their plans. Most of the building materials were ready, the site would be huge. We should have plenty of work for at least two months. The driver started the engine and we left. The commissioner showed me a village before us. There were three others around the vast field. Perhaps in a few years it would all become one big city.

In the village a man was waiting for us. The Commissar spoke to him in Russian while the driver walked away. We continued walking to a house.

- Well, here is where I live for the moment. I want to build a bigger house next door because with this huge project I will definitely stay here for a long time. Do you have professionals able to build this house?

So that was what he wanted to ask me in confidence. I gave it some thought before before giving my consent. The Commissar introduced me to the director of the village and the kolkhoz. He would supervise the building of the new house. He spoke enough German to make himself understood. That was very good for me: "My men will start tomorrow."

Back at camp, I told Bernard that we would meet with his team after the soup to speak about a future building site in the village, asking for his complete discretion. He brought his masons, his carpenters and even his architecture student. Together we walked away as if to take a short stroll to the camp's central square.

- Remember when we built a house for the commander of our first camp? Well, starting tomorrow you'll do it again, building a house in a village, actually it's a kolkhoz. The director there will provide all the equipment and building materials. But under no circumstance speak about this to anyone, neither here nor on our future building site!

- Okay, sir.

- In the meantime enjoy this fine spring evening. Do you remember when I left the hospital? I told you that when I said goodbye the director wished me a 'good winter'! He knew what he was talking about! Well, my dear comrades, we're now in late May and we are still here, unharmed. My father had repeated this to me at each each of my furloughs: "My son, we know that this Austrian corporal will never win the war. Pray to God that you come back to us." and he always added: "Just get home alive, my son. We will do the rest."

Bernard then said:

- Lieutenant, you have been a great father to us. But why did your father called him 'the Austrian corporal'?

- Good question, Bernard. My father never mentioned Hitler's name. He was anti-Nazi and very religious as all the family and we can say, the entire Fulda area. Thanks to him I followed the same path. That is my strength. You understood ever since we knew each other that faith in God is the most effective protection!

- But sir, why do we never talk about your youth?

- It's because I stayed the same. And I will remain like this all in my life!

*

The next day the commissar was waiting for us on his 'unofficial' site. He had arranged for his driver to take us every morning to the village where I would stay with my team while he would go back to direct the work for the car manufacturing site.

The director of the kolkhoz came back with the task of ensuring our lunch.

Even at the risk of belaboring the point I repeated the instruction to my team: "Never speak to anyone, absolutely no one about your work here. If someone asks you what you are doing in the village answer that you were digging wells for the water supply of the kolkhoz. Do not take my warnings lightly, I would not want us to finish our life together in a 'forced labor camp' from where no one ever comes back!"

I think this time they understood. For three weeks the team was doing a remarkable job. The manager was full of praise for these tireless workers and professionalism of the Germans. He told me that the commissar came to eat soup every night at his home without ever forgetting to go to see the progress of his new home.

I congratulated my team and especially the young architect who although not yet graduated was very good. He completed all plans in time. From the outside, the house was indistinguishable from the others. One had to go inside to discover a level of comfort that was very unusual here at the time. In the middle of the main room a fire place could heat the whole house. There was also a separate sleeping area, a table and four chairs for meals but no stove because the food was provided by the kolkhoz. However, we had provided a bathroom complete with sink, toilet and shower plus a mirror. My team had dug a water well. The director had provided the bathroom fixtures and the mirror but we made the table, the chairs and the three windows. The last day of work, around 4pm, the director and the Commissar came to see the new house. The Commissar could not have been more satisfied and congratulated the entire team. "When I leave, it will be your home!" He said something to the manager to get something and returned with a woman carrying two trays laden with food and drink. He regaled us with a real treat, three buttered toast for each, cheese, onions and a glass of vodka. My team was thrilled, compliments abounded on all sides, including from the director's wife.

With that the commissar's chauffeur drove us to the last truck heading back to camp. Obviously, the other prisoners wanted to know why we were coming after all. Bernard responded very natural that we wanted to finish the construction of wells for the future camp and that the commissar was especially moved to thank us but tomorrow we would be back with the group.

We still spent four weeks to complete the camp. The fence was lined with two rows of barbed wire. Every 50 yards there was a watchtower equipped with projectors. Actually it looked like a real fortress. The new barracks were a real surprise for us. While we were away at the village the other teams had been directed to dig trenches 40 feet long, 30 feet wide and six feet deep,with steps going down Then all this was covered by a make-shift roof that rested on the level ground. We were all taken aback by this strange way of providing space, especially Wilhelm. He tried to get some clarification from the Russian engineers but all they said was that it was temporary because and they were in a hurry because many prisoners would be leaving soon. And, indeed, the commissar informed us that we would leave the camp in two days. Only my team would stay a little longer until after most of the prisoners would be transferred elsewhere.

The remaining work was for cleaning the camp, completing gates with barbed wire and building two guard posts. Before boarding the last truck, the commissar quietly informed me that the next day early in the afternoon his driver would come for me. He saw my surprise and told me to keep quiet.

What did he want now? I racked my brains but I could find no explanation for this arrangement. You only have to wait.

As always, my friends were curious:

"What will we do now? We were doing fine here. And what is our new destination?"

- Consider taking a shower, go eat and enjoy the sweetness of the evening. I'll go see the commander to try to learn a little more and I'll let you know.

The commander and I shared a very good vegetable soup with potatoes and more than three slices of white bread. Knowing him, I saw in his face that the news would not be very good. He begins by saying that for me and my team a new activity is planned. In two days a column of trucks will come for us and will bring us to a new destination. He does not know where or what our new task would be:

- As you know, in the Soviet Union nothing is fixed. I myself probably will change my camp in a month or so. A hundred prisoners will remain here for camp cleaning, disinfecting and for building new latrines. In three weeks new prisoners will arrive and a new commander will probably be appointed before that date. We'll see you before you leave.

On entering my hut all eyes were on me.

- Well dear comrades, the commander told me that we leave the day after tomorrow for a new camp and a new activity. He does not know any more than that. It's the Soviet system. No communication between the camps. There is nothing else to do than to enjoy a little moment of tranquility, some good food and the sweetness of the summer evenings.

*

The next day the driver picked me up to meet with the commissar at the camp's north entrance. From there we headed to the south gate where the driver left us alone.

- Come to witness the arrival of the traitors to our country.

What was he talking about? He then told me about the Vlasov army who had been created by the German army for Russian deserters who volunteered to fight alongside the Germans against the Red Army, hoping that the Germans would win the war and that Vlasov would become the new tsar of Russia.

- 5000 of these traitors were captured in Czechoslovakia and are now coming here. There had been many more of them but many of them have already died in labor camps.

The conversation is interrupted by a noise. The gates are opened to let a herd of men enter who all move with great difficulty. The guards were shouting: "Dawai! Dawai!" striking the prisoners who had trouble keeping up. I quickly understood why they dragged their feet: they were chained together, a metal band around the ankles. These men were no more than skin and bones, dressed in rags, filthy dirty with grime and obviously very thirsty. Then the guards pushed them into the bottoms of these special huts dug into the ground that we had found so intrigueing. The guards then withdrew the make-shift roofs and some prisoners were ordered to bury the 'traitors' alive. During all this I felt the commissar watching me. No longer able to restrain myself I asked him why he wanted to show me this monstrosity.

- Look, I'm still very young. I was not in the war while I finished my studies in the political military academy. But I can not accept this criminal act. Let them shoot traitors but not this. If you have the chance to get out of here alive remember what you just saw. Later, when the world has changed you can tell them that you witnessed these crimes with your own eyes.

I was stunned.

- We are not all monsters or criminals. Let them know that, too.
- Who gave the order?
- This comes from very high. Never tell anyone about this while you are still a prisoner here. The commander did not ask any questions because he knows the system. If your comrades ask you just tell them that the Commissar wanted to see you one last time to personally thank you for your excellent work and that he wishes you good luck.

I have spoken to no one about this incredible crime and only repeated to my comrades the stock phrase of the Commissar.

*

CHAPTER 13

Will This Ever Stop?

Where would our umpteenth transfer take us? Neither the delegate nor the commander knew where we were being sent. For the present both men preferred to think about our short term well being: a good soup and three slices of bread in the morning before the trucks would arrive and four slices of bread for the trip. The commander told me to urge my team mates to drink a lot while water was still available.

A question was burning my lips: there were plenty of other team leaders but why was the commander always speaking to me?

- Here in the Soviet Union you have to be absolutely sure who you can trust. This is an issue of huge importance in our lives. Here one is suspicious of everything and everyone. Now the good news: your delegate, Ladislav, worked all night to sort the latest Red Cross postcards that arrived last night. Fortunately, in U.S.S.R. we record everything.

- Will our records be given to the commander of the new camp?

- In principle, yes, provided there is someone in charge to receive them.

- Ladislav gave me the reply cards for my team and one that was addressed to me personally. It was in the hand of my mother in Gothic script. After various news, she concluded with these words: "Your return is in the hands of God. We pray every day for you and hope that the Blessed Virgin Mary protects you." I was happy to receive this maternal encouragement. True, God and the Blessed Virgin have never abandoned me.

All my friends had received a card except one from East Prussia. He knew that his family left their city before the arrival of the Red Army to take refuge with cousins near Hamburg. But he did not know their new address. I comforted him as best I could.

The day went by quietly. In the evening, I was asked to see the commander.

- Let's have dinner together. I want to tell you that I like Ladislav and his way to deal with you and me and I hope he will come with me if I am transferred elsewhere. All prisoners leave the camp tomorrow morning for a new destination. A hundred new prisoners should arrive here in a few days. This is an opportunity to have the camp cleaned thoroughly. Subsequently, the health service will arrive to check several thousand prisoners who continue your work on the site.

The phone was ringing. Good news: the commander remains in place, and so will Ladislav. It is the chief commissar for the project that has received the confirmation from the regional director of the GPU. Given the vastness and importance of the site he needs the current commander for continuity.

All this puts us in a good mood for our meal. What exactly did Ladislav and the commander know about what was really happening? This intrigued me and I steered the conversation in that direction. It turned out that they had no idea. They believed everything was just fine.

- Yes, commander, your commissar is still very young but he is keen to do a good job with this immense project. It will take several years. This means that if you want to stay here any length of time you have to cultivate a good relationship with him.

On the way to my hut, I thought of the next groups of prisoners who would be building new barracks on the mass grave of the 5000 soldiers of the Vlasov army. Later, when those barracks would become useless, a new city would be built above the same place. The brave young commissar and I were the only ones who would know it.

*

The next day at about 9am a row of trucks is waiting for us with a pack of brutal guards to 'help' us climb inside. Thirty prisoners and two guards per vehicle. We drove for about three hours under a blazing sun before reaching a swampy area. On the left a line of unfinished railroad tracks, on the right a country road that led to a camp site without barracks. Instead we could see tents, each accommodating fifty men. The enclosure of the camp was marked by a simple barbed wire fence. The whole place seemed like something provisional, but why?

I had no time to think about it because with barking their odious "Dawai! Dawai! Dawai! " the guards chased us from the trucks accompanied by shots and blows to encourage us to rush to the tents. All my team mates wanted to follow me but there was not enough room in any one of the tents. There was nothing in the tents except a tarp on the dirt floor.

In the tents the heat was torrid. Two hours later, no one had shown up. We were left to suffocate in this oven. No longer willing to suffer like this I opened the tent wide. A young guard appeared pointing his Kalashnikov at me and screaming. I replied in German with the same shouting voice: "I want to see the commander!" while making the sign of the cross as if to bless him. He looks at me like I am an alien from outer space and fled the scene as if he had seen the devil. Of course, this shouting contest had brought many people out of their tents and everybody was yelling: "Commander! Commander!"

Finally, a Russian officer shows up flanked by two guards. He wants to speak with a tent leader. I identify myself and we leave together but without guards. This officer speaks enough German for me to make myself understood. At the camp entrance we enter a small shack that serves as his make-shift office. Several open boxes with files attract my attention. Were they ours? The officer nods. Our former commander had passed them on since they must accompany us throughout our captivity.

- You will stay here for two days and then you will be directed to another camp that is almost finished with barracks for a hundred prisoners each. I will follow you there and these tents will be taken down.

- Are there any supplies, sir?

- During these two days trucks will deliver them at about noon. You will have soup, bread and water. Since you do not work, the food is simple but adequate.

- Thank you, sir.

*

The new camp was huge, at least 10,000 prisoners! At the entrance stood the officer that I had met two days ago. He is now our camp commander and is accompanied by a stranger. I gave them my military salute and to my surprised he returned it.

One point for me. I quickly brought my team to the third hut that looked like all the others we passed.

I went right away to meet the commander and the stranger who accompanied him. He is a Pole born in East Prussia. He was captured in 1944 and speaks German and Russian very well. He is 24 and is called Friedrich.

- You are Friedrich? This is a German name!

- Yes, and my brothers and sisters also have German names. My father had a farm and worked with the Germans before the war. He greatly enjoyed them. When Hitler attacked Poland he was drafted into the Polish army and taken prisoner. Thanks to his good relations with his Prussian neighbors he was released quickly.

I was amazed by the size of the camp.

-Yes, but there are really three camps, each with its own commander. The prisoners of two of our camps work in Kharkov, a few miles from here, to rebuild the city. It was almost entirely destroyed in the war. Our camp will finish the highway to the city and rebuild the rail tracks. At the moment we have problems because we do not have enough tools. They were promised a long time ago but as usual they have not arrived. By the way, we have a well equipped hospital to deal with all three camps.

- Thanks a lot, Friedrich. Now I understand the situation.

- Another thing: soon the commander will ask each team leader for a list of all his prisoners. Here is some writing paper and a pencil so that you can show up well prepared.

- Thanks a lot, Friedrich. When are we expected?

- In an hour from now.

He looks at his watch. It is noon, on August 9 of 1946.

Drawing up my list I find that I have a dozen newcomers. I meant to introduce myself to them but then I remembered that this may be useless. News, all kind of news, travelled fast in these camps.

August showed its heat. We have to work ten hours a day on the road, while the other half of the prisoners take care of the railway. The food? A thin soup in the morning with two slices of black bread. We reserved a portion for the day. In the evening, the same menu. We were entitled to two fifteen minute breaks to drink water. Our muscles melted like snow in the sun.

I told Friedrich about the food and the inevitable decline of our ability to perform our tasks.

- You know the 'norms' system?

- Yes, Friedrich, we know that system very well but did you see what kind of tools we have! How can anyone make a solid road with that stuff while we are hungry?

171

- Solid? Who spoke of a 'solid' road? You have to build a road, period. Just a road.

- Thanks, Friedrich, I got the message, that's great!

The next day I met all the team leaders to remind them of the importance of the 'norms' and the need for us to make progress with the road. "From now, let's move our German work standards down a notch. The quality of our work will come back when we will have the right tools and some better food."

Miraculously, we went twice as fast and promptly received official compliments. I told them about our work on the site of the future Fiat car factory 'Togliattigrad' under the command of a political commissar: first the basics of the road and then with a steam roller we made it solid. He said that with a smile. That was exactly what we are doing here.

I reported this conversation to Friedrich and the commander. "All that's left to do for you is to wait for your next rations!" the commander told us with a smile. For the three following days we do not see any change. I complained to our site manager stressing that my men were totally exhausted. Friedrich told me that the site manager had called the commander to tell him that since we had exceeded the standards we absolutely earned better food.

In perfect Soviet style we got smiles, angry phone calls, the usual promises and then ..... nothing!

Slowly slurping our thin soup we remain outside, enjoying the mild evening air. One night I suddenly hear someone call me by my name. I see a man, a very thin guy, almost ghostly. At first, his features don't tell me anything but then in a flash I know, amazed:

- Helmut? It is you, Helmut?

- Yes, I'm recovering, I left the hospital, I was very sick.

- Have you already eaten?

- Yes, yes, and I wanted to take a small stroll through the camp just in case, I would find an acquaintance. You know I've often thought of you.

I introduced him to my team telling them about our first meeting in Brno and how he was responsible for the train wagon just in front of ours.

- You know, Helmut, many of the men here were in my wagon then and now we are a cohesive team. It's your turn to tell us about your experiences.

In a faltering voice, as if searching for words or his memories, he began his story:

- Remember our conversation in this vast prairie that we crossed on that wretched train? When we were separated getting on the train, you told me: may God protect you. And I answered you with the same words. With those words: "May God protect you" you have given me the strength to survive.

His journey was the same hell as for us all. Death, thirst, corpses piling up. Things differed only on one point:

"When the train stopped to allow us to bathe in the river unfortunately, my fellow prisoners and I had time to drink before the guards shot into the air and howled at us to get back into the wagons. The result was a terrible dysentery. Initially, when the shit ran down our legs I was paralyzed with shame. I was not alone. Once, during a stop, I saw you from a distance making the sign of the cross on five or six dead bodies before the guards made you go back in the car. I knew you were very religious. I have never forgotten this vision. We followed your advise to eat dry peas and it stopped my dysentery. The others all died.

When the train arrived in the Donbass from the original hundred prisoners 73 were dead, only 22 survived. We may have set some kind of record. Four other comrades and I were too weak to get up and to get out of the car. We waited for death. We did not have enough strength to call for help. I thought about you and I prayed simply with what little energy I had. Suddenly, I heard Russian. Men come up to the wagon, take a look inside and start yelling. Later four soldiers come up. They saw that I was an officer and they took me down first. There were still two others with me but then I heard two shots behind me. The last two had been killed. While they gave us water to drink I could see the last prisoners going to a camp."

- That was us. I looked up into your car but could not see anything as we were marched to the camp. We were the last.

" Some other prisoners were recovered from the cars, very sick like us. The Russians loaded us on a truck and we went to a prison hospital. On arrival we were given a kind of sweet porridge and even after washing it down with water it had the taste of some strange tea. Nurses helped us to remove our rotted clothes leaving our papers in our hand, and then a shower. Oh my God, what a pleasure! We were sent to the medical service. As I began to lose consciousness they took us to the hospital and laid us on a bed. After that I do not remember anything. After a few days I felt better and with thirty-four prisoners considered cured we rode very far on three trucks to this place. The camp was smaller then, perhaps for 3000 prisoners. On my truck coming here there was a group of officers who were loudly arguing about the attack on Hitler in 1944."

- What do you mean? I don't understand.

He thought for a while making a great effort to restore his memory of what he had heard back then.

"Well, for example, there was one who commented on the attack against Hitler saying something like: 'At that critical moment in our history we should have focussed all our efforts on the final victory but instead there were these traitors from the German nobility who were determined to remove our head of state at the most important time in our homeland's history. This was a crime against Germany.' Another added: 'The war was not over. We had a secret weapon to crush the enemy. These traitors gave information to our enemies to bomb the site where we had them. We had the first supersonic aircraft. They were unbeatable! It was all sabotaged by some engineers who were traitors.'

A third guy told about his experience in France after the invasion of the Allied in Normandy. 'The French were squabbling among themselves about their difference in politics instead of supporting Hitler's grand ideas of a united Europe like Napoleon had tried to achieve. Instead in their hatred of us Germans they kept blowing up trains, especially the communists with their guerilla warfare, and so on.' I was bewildered by all this Nazis garbage!"

- What was your first job after arriving at the camp?

"We immediately started to clear the city of Kharkov, virtually by hand. It was very hard. The commander and his men were pushing us relentlessly. They screamed all day: Dawai! Dawai! hitting us all the time with their rifle butts. The food was a thin soup in the morning and in the evening with a slice of black bread. As we were already malnourished our work force diminished day by day."

- Did you see the Nazi officers again?

"Yes, only one and he had lost his arrogance. The reality of POW life was beginning to break him. I think it was around October when more than half of the prisoners were sick and unable to work. The director responsible for the Kharkov district asked for a reason and our commander replied it was for lack of food. And very soon our camp received supplemental food. Two weeks later we were back at work. Winter took us by surprise. The people of Kharkov, or rather the survivors who lived in cellars, rebelled against the slow pace of reconstruction, not to mention the totally inadequate supplies of food and building materials. To our surprise our Russian guards started to attack their own people and chased them back into their cellars like rats! This made me pity them. I still cannot understand this Soviet system.

We received warmer clothes but towards the middle of December I was totally burnt out. I was very sick and with other prisoners. I was transported to a hospital on the outskirts of Kharkov. As there were no drugs very few of us survived! I prayed every day and I finally got better in late January. In mid-February I left the hospital and came back here to resume my work. Much of the city had been cleared and we were able to start the actual rebuilding. Our food had improved and the work progressed well. In March, we built a second camp for 3000 prisoners. Our work was always focused on Kharkov where we made good progress. In late May we completed an entire neighborhood and the Governor handed the keys of the houses to the people who had lived in caves for so long. What surprised me was the layout of the apartments. There was a kitchen, a toilet and a lobby connecting four small two-room apartments to these common facilities.That meant there was no privacy! In mid-July, a third camp was added to the other two and we started building a sizable hospital."

I told him about us:

- We arrived here in early August. We are currently working on the construction project called 'Road and Rail' to improve transportation to and from Kharkov..

- When I am completely healed can I come to your team or at least to your camp?

- I promise to do everything to have you with us.

Later, I talked with Friedrich and the commander. Helmut was appointed officer in charge of a barrack and his team worked alongside ours.

*

We were in the middle of August and everything worked like clockwork: we were always exceeding the standards, got better quality food and our morale was high. Our road was only two miles from the camp. It was rumored that in two weeks we would get a steamroller to strengthen it.

One evening Friedrich wanted to talk to me. There were some unexpected developments. A new political commissar had just arrived and he had a long conversation with the commander. I was having dinner with him that evening and got some rather disturbing news:

- Our work projects were taken over by a political commissar. Our former project manager was deemed ineffective and too forgiving with the prisoners.

- And where is our project manager now?

No comments, but his frowning said it all. In such a ruthless regime as the Soviet system the life of a man is not worth much when he had the misfortune to displease!

The next morning the barracks leaders were introduced to our new site boss. He sounded just like a true specimen of his trade, in his forties, nothing like our previous site manager.

He addressed us in Russian with a translator trying to make sense out of this man's ranting. This man made it sound as if we had not worked very hard and that we had even sabotaged the road project. The 'norms' would be revised upwards and we should catch up by working twice as hard. In total confusion we looked at each other unsure what to make of this avalance of accusations. Helmut, who was not far from me, looked at me with a shrug. As our dismay was obvious enough for the commissar to notice and he asked us in perfect German whether his message was clear. I addressed him:

- Comrade Commissar, we did not understand what you are saying.

There followed a barrage of curses at the translator who quickly made his exit from the scene. Then the captain speaks directly to us in a more pallatable tone:

- You are prisoners of war and you must pay for all damage your army has done to our country. Right now you have to build a road and a railway to Kharkov. You gave us a dirt road, not a highway. In late September, with heavy rains, this road will be impassable. We must strenthen and solidify this route. Tomorrow half of you will go to a quarry to break stones, load them and bring them here. The other half will immediately begin to rebuild the road. For now, continue to clear the way. I don't give a damn about standards. All I want is that the road is passable before the end of

September even if you have to work from morning to night and from night to morning.

- Helmut, I think we will have some hard weeks ahead of us!

We lost all the benefits granted by the former head of the construction site. All prisoners had to be on the site at 8am and leave at 6pm. That meant we had to start from camp at 7am. As there was a small food supply in the reserve, the commander gave the order that the kitchen would reduce the quality of the soup gradually. He made one last recommendation: "Never tell the commissar that you are a believer!"

*

Wake up at 6am, soup, bread, and at 7, a group of new guards with "Dawai! Dawai! Dawai!". We arrive at the work site totally out of breath. Some of the prisoners are taken by truck to the quarry where the Russians have already used dynamite to break the rock. Under sweltering heat and with only lukewarm water as food our comrades must cut these stones in large blocks with medieval tools.

As for us we continue working on our dirt road, 'encouraged' by the screams of the guards. From time to time, a so-called 'engineer' passes by to control who knows what and disappears giving us a wink of his eye. "If this guy is an engineer, I'm cardiologist like my father," quips Helmut. Nobody is in the mood to laugh. The water they supplied is lukewarm. Before drinking, I take advantage of a moment when the guards look the other way to clean my tin can. Some comrades are doing the same and one of the prisoners not on my team is surprised by a guard who immediately descends on him with kicks and rifle butts. Others chase us from the water bucket and order us to resume work immediately. "Come, Helmut, we'll take care of this guy." Our guards do not see it that way. Seeing our comrade bleeding, unable to get up, I start screaming too, and Helmut and all other also scream in unison. The 'engineer' shows up to see what's happening. When he sees the state of our comrade he gives the order to return to work assuring us in barely understandable German that the injured will be taken to the hospital.

Upon my return to the camp I told Friedrich about the incident. He found out that no one with injuries was admitted to the hospital. Incidentally, Friedrich told me that our German doctor was no longer here but in Kharkov with Russian doctors to establish the new civil hospital.

Together we head to the commander to tell him about the incident. He listens to me and picks up the phone. The conversation is in Russian and is not long, his account even less. "Listen, your friend has been taken over by the GPU and is currently in a specialized hospital. My only response was "May God grant him eternal peace". The commander said nothing. I thanked him and we left. I advised Friedrich: "Not a word of it to anyone. The commander trusted us."

In the barracks everyone could see that the soup had gained quite a bit of 'clarity'. Too bad! After a slice of bread the team felt better. Helmut came to visit, we talked in a somber fashion. I felt a growing anxiety among my comrades. I had to say something:

- My fellow galley slaves, the change of manager has resulted in a monumental change of our conditions. This new political commissar is a true product of the Soviet system. He received his orders and he knows very well that he runs a big risk if he does not reach the goals. And without us, that is impossible. He needs us.

Helmut lightened up a bit. I offered to walk back to his barracks with him. On the way he asked me what had become of the prisoner that had been beaten.

- From what I was told he is in a hospital in Kharkov,.

Helmut did not pursue his question. Was he deceived?

- You know, Aloÿs, we are in serious trouble. The commissar and his thugs make me feel very frightened. In their eyes we are just a bunch of criminals who have invaded and destroyed their country and we have to pay for it.

- Helmut, yes, you're right but the dead cannot pay anything. They need us alive. Keep our trust in God and in us. Our comrades need us. Set a good example.

Our work was becoming increasingly difficult. With the lack of food and only a little warm water to sip all day we trudged back to the camp as if we were re-enacating the 'stations of the cross'.

Now the first of us were succombing to these deprivations. In each barrack a dozen men or so were no longer able to get up for work. I informed Friedrich. The commander came to inspect some barracks. The next morning a sanitary commission appeared and confirmed that these prisoners were no longer able to work.

The steamroller had finally arrived on our site but our comrades were dropping like flies, one after the other in the middle of the site. We went to get water, we helped them up and I drank water, too. The water had a strange taste. I immediately warned my friends: Do not drink it! I shout with all my strength by asking my friends to join me at the water barrel. The guards bark at us, pointing their guns and order us to return to work immediately. We drown their "Dawai"! with our "Niet! Niet". The 'engineer' happens to pass by and yells his orders to the guards to leave.

I ask him to look at the barrel and to taste a bit of its liquid. He refuses to even do as much as to wet his lip with his rotten water and prefers to seek out the commissar. Okay, but hurry! Suddenly, a terrible weakness overcomes me. I lose control over my body. Helmut finds out, he shakes me: "Aloÿs, our road will stop here. We will all die." Three other barracks officials confirm his prognosis just looking at me. In my agony I make a distress call to God and the Virgin Mary that they do not abandon me.

The commissar arrived. He saw my sign of the cross. He leans on the barrel, he smells the foul odor. I feel I am regaining my strength and before the commissar has opened his mouth I tell him:

- Comrade Commissar, your guards have not renewed the water at all for a long time. It has become a poison. We prisoners are treated as war criminals. We are hungry and thirsty and this is all we have to drink. I can tell you that tonight most of us will be sick, poisoned, and many will die. So tell me: who are the criminals? Your gang of brutes are treating us worse than animals, but we are human beings, and we are not criminals. Wherever we have worked, either in the mines or on many other projects, we have done a good job and we were respected. You want work done, treat us humanely! Once, we had a commissar who abused us, even killed some of us. We made sure he was arrested by the regional branch of the GPU.

- I am ordering every available truck to take you back to camp.

Then he left. Helmut said, "Aloÿs you have an inner strength and a will that I do not have. You talked to the commissar in a calm and fair voice and I think he will no longer harm us. You are very much like your comrades have described you."

Eyes closed I thanked my divine protectors muttering: "Lord, let me keep my faith. It will protect me and guide me along my life path."

When the first trucks arrived, most of us were lying on the ground in agony. I told Helmut and other officers to take care of the weakest first. The trucks left without guards! We were not more than fifty left on the site, plus those working in the quarry. I started to walk back and when we were halfway the trucks came back for us. Friedrich was with them leading the return of the remaining prisoners. Later we will go to see the commander. Helmut came to me:

- So Aloÿs, good news from Friedrich?

- Helmut, we won a human battle. Our Soviets discovered something of a peaceful revolution, unknown in this country. But for now another battle begins for the weakest among us, that of survival!

- I think it applies to us all of us, weak or strong.

Half my team was sick. Fifteen men had already been hospitalized due to severe diarrhea, fever and a state of extreme weakness. Ludwig, the cook, who had not yet started his work had never seen anything like it: "At the hospital they do not know where to turn and they had orders from outside authorities to do the everything possible to save the sick." From the outside? What could that mean? Who gave the orders?

I heard the last trucks arriving. Still more sick? Men emerge, breathless, distraught. Friedrich was not with them. Helmut was coming out of the commander's office: "He wants to see you."

- Okay, but first my friends.

The commander shook my hand when I walked into his office. Helmut told him about the events of the day.

- Let me congratulate you for your courage. The commissar phoned to inform me. He was worried. He also said he fired the engineer and the guards and he phoned the hospital. Starting right now my camp will receive the necessary food. Two trucks have already been unloaded and the kitchens is working at full speed to prepare a good soup.

I returned to my team with the good news. Another column of trucks entered the camp, this time also with Friedrich. They were our comrades from the quarry. They dragged themselves to their barracks. We had to send a large number of them directly to the hospital. Friedrich told me, "I'm on it, you go back to tell the commander".

Helmut and other officials were already there. The commander telephoned. He was very much on edge:

- I just told the commissar to get health personnel with disinfectants and to clean the mattresses. The hospital is full. We need to move some prisoners to take over four or five barracks near the hospital that are under construction. Upon leaving here you give the order to the able-bodied men to go to the kitchen for soup, bread and water. No food for the patients, the hospital will take care of them. You, too, should get something to eat but do it quickly because a large amount of organizational work is ahead.

He then assigned the tasks: Friedrich, Helmut and I were to go to the current hospital and start the construction of new barracks. Others were to get the prisoners out of the contaminated five barracks and transfer them to some empty barracks. I had never seen a camp commander in such a state of anxiety. I felt that all the penned-up hatred for the commissar had boiled over in him. He ended with these words:

- Once the first of the new barracks is ready it will be occupied by 41 hospitalized invalids and several amputees awaiting their departure for Germany.

What? This surprise statement did not fall on deaf ears! Here is your chance to be part of this convoy, I said to myself!

*

Chapter 14

My long Way back to my Life at Home

We went to work: five barracks to be emptied, disinfected, and forty new mattresses to be procured. Meanwhile, the other barrack leaders rearranged their men's space assignments throughout the camp. Fortunately the kitchen served us an another portion of a very thick soup. That was what kept us going. At midnight the commander finally released us from our frantic pace: "Go to sleep now. See you tomorrow morning at 6 for the transfer of all the sick and disabled."

For us it was a very short night. I quickly drew up a plan to create work details for the transfer of the weakest of the patients to the hospital and to separate those that were already out of danger. I sent Friedrich, Helmut and another officer to get stretchers. We ran across a male nurse and Friedrich tells him in Russian about our mission. He seemed surprised and is afraid to get involved. Nothing to do but to wait. Another man in a white coat appeared, a doctor. He speaks German and I explained that things had changed at the camp and that the commander had instructed us to do this work at the hospital.

- Do you understand, Doctor?

- Yes, yes. That suits us fine because we do not know where to put all the sick. They must have food poisoning. Their symptoms are all the same: diarrhea, fever, and they do not want to eat anything. We already have exhausted our stock of diarrhea medicines but I have already ordered a big new supply.

- Do not give them water but charred bread! It is a simple but effective way to stop diarrhea.

- You are right, I'll get on it right away.

- Wait a second, how many doctors do you have here?

- Two, but I have contacted the hospitals in Kharkov asking for more, given this situation.

- You did well because there are still more sick in the camp. For now I suggest that we carry the worst of them to one of the barracks we prepared for them.

- We must get more barracks ready for them. The maximum allowed for each barrack is 30 patients.

- How many of them do you have here already?

- For now 42, most of them injured in work accidents. They have been waiting already three weeks to be sent back to Germany.

- Then we will put twelve of the patients that are out of immediate danger to the second barracks.

- Very good.

It took the entire day to move the sick into the hospital. We came and went between our dying comrades, trying to ease their delirium. Some of them had suffered through amputations, moved from one hospital to another. One had lost a foot another a leg, another an arm. All of them were in deplorable conditions. They had suffered a lot and were still suffering. A German doctor had been able to repair some of the damage done by their earlier crude treatment. All along they were kept waiting for their promised return to Germany.

Utterly exhausted, we returned to our barracks in the evening. Helmut and I suddenly felt overwhelmed and nauseated. My head was spinning and I vomited. The ground gave way under me and I lost consciousness.

*

Two bulbs dimly illuminated the room where I came to again. I tried in vain to get my bearings. Apparently, there were other patients around me. Exhausted, I went back to sleep. Someone woke me up. A white blouse touches my forehead and slipped a thermometer under my arm. No sudden movements, please! I still remembered the broken thermometer ... The nurse removes the thermometer and made a note of my temperature - and my fate as she sees it.

The room was become awake with activity. Nurses made their rounds. Some patients were delirious. Prisoners that were out of danger acted as orderlies trying their best to wash their patients as well as they could and cleaning their soiled mattresses, scenes I had already experienced before. Here we had more resources, the quality of care was better, everything was as clean as it could be.

Helmut comes to see me together with the commander and Friedrich. He gives me my wallet back. The commander says he had seen the doctor and is aware of my condition. What worries them is my fever, still almost 105°. The commander tries to reassure me by blaming my collapse on the events of recent weeks that had been too tough for me. The arrival of the doctor interrupts the visit. I knew him already but not the lovely nurse who companied him. I say to myself "here again is my guardian angel!"

A blonde, even with lipstick and eyes of intense blue! "This is your nurse, Irina. She will take good care of you. We will do our best to get you back on your feet quickly. The commander has great respect for you."

Irina gives me medicine and leaning towards me, whispers that a commission will soon come to select patients to be sent back to

Germany along with the amputees. I try to absorb this message without fully grasping its meaning.

Irina was troubled. The fever had decreased but not my utter state of exhaustion. It remained insurmountable. My survival instinct seemed to have left me.

When she came back for another visit she looked to me more like a ghost. Everything I saw appeared like unreal. When Irina saw me in this state she ran for the doctor who gave me an injection. I fell back to a deep sleep. When I opened my eyes during the night Irina was at my bedside and told me that the fever had completely stopped. "Now I'll take care of you." Again she whispered in my ear: "So that you will see your family again", punctuating her words with a furtive but ever so gentle caress on my cheek. What joy! How comforting! I felt protected. Yes, my guardian angel was watching over me!

Some patients that were almost healed began to serve the soup. Irina wanted to give me a sweet porridge. I had no appetite and it is only for obedience sake that I swallowed some of it. Then she gave me a powder to be taken with tea. It was meant to help me sleep. Before leaving she said:

- You have to find some disease that cannot be diagnosed. You're a believer, right? Then pray.

- Irina, how do you know this?

- Yesterday in your sleep you joined hands and it seemed to me that you were praying.

- Thanks Irina, you really are my guardian angel.

She did not understand but she gave me a smile.

Some of my comrades around me ate with gusto but many others refused their meal with a simple nod. Those had given up and were letting themselves die, no more strength, no more will to live. I wanted to help them through prayer and some words of encouragement. I felt myself more alive. I sank into deep sleep.

A terrible stomach pain woke me up and I cried out in pain. What was happening now? In the twilight I recognize Irina's silhouette. She leans toward me and said: "Now you're going back to Germany for sure." But why? "Now you have a disease that no one can diagnose. I will give you a sleep medication."

Alone again, remorse assailed me. My conscience told me that I should not desert my fellow prisoners and my responsibility to help them in their need. On the other hand, was it not right that I would think about my own survival? What prisoner was not thinking about his survival? Everything was blurred in my mind. I was not able to put this right and I finally fell asleep. When I woke again I was moaning in agony. My stomach ache had not left me. Vaguely, I saw a shadow passing by. Who was this?

In the morning I asked Irina about it. She replied with a smile:

- Now, for sure, you will be on the list of those to be sent back.

- How did that happen, Irina?

- Yesterday we had to provide a list of patients with symptoms that would show their inability to work. The shadow you saw tonight was that of an official who was to check on the state of health of those patients that were in hopeless decline. Your groans when he passed saved you.

Helmut came to visit.

- We have learned that the amputees and a number of other patients will soon leave for Germany. The commander told Friedrich to inform you. I pray for you to be among them. Do not worry about us or your team. I will take over. Everything is going well at the construction site, have no fear. Excuse me but I can not stay longer and I will not return. The commander says it's too dangerous to come see you. Arousing the commission's suspicion could undo everything. Let us trust in God.

Irina looked cheerful:

- You are on the list!

Did I understand this right? With an intense prayer I was thanking Our Lady and my guardian angel for helping me to survive to see my parents again, maybe soon.

Irina still brought me her sweet porridge and tea. I drank it happily and dutifully ate a little of the kascha mush but still without any appetite. Irina took charge: "You have to eat, you're too skinny. Otherwise you'll never live to see Germany. Only two more days to wait."

I could not believe it. My life as a soldier and prisoner had taught me a deep distrust of everything and everybody. In the Soviet Union nothing could ever be taken for granted. Everything could change from one minute to the next for no reason.

Irina came back at night to give me strawberries and cream. She forced me to eat it all. "You have to eat here because during the transport there will definitely not be any food."

"Yes Irina you're right, but I still have these awful doubts whether I will really see my homeland again."

*

In the early hours of the next day the orderlies came to help us to make our toilet and to distribute old Red Army uniforms with hats featuring the ubiquitous red star.

Hobbling to support the amputees we went for one last prisoners' meal. Irina gave me her sweet porridge and encouraged everyone to eat. I drank a lot of tea and took a trip to the latrine which - surprise - was very clean. Irina was waiting for me. She had tears in her eyes and kissed me: "You must pray a lot, it will help you. I've never prayed. I don't know how."

Stealthily she slipped a few slices of bread under my coat wrapped in a piece of clean white cloth with my tin and my spoon and a wire to put around my waist to hook things on. In the single coat pocket was my wallet. I was ready and so were the others but nothing was happening, we just stood there.

Why the delay? Gradually, uncertainty changed into fear. What if all this was staged to expose anyone who had faked his disability? The anguish put my stomach in knots. It was like getting stabbed in the stomach. It made me scream in pain. Irina immediately runs to me accompanied by the doctor who gave me a powder to ease the pain. Irina does not leave my side. A stranger comes, the head of our convoy. He exchanges a few words in

Russian with the nurse and then leaves. He wanted to know if she thought I was transportable and, of course, Irina said there was no problem.

Suddenly things seem to get under way. The amputees and the sick prisoners, 62 in all, are separated into groups. The trucks are there. Doctors and nurses distribute a certificate to each of us. This is a document from the Red Cross, in Russian and German, with our name, rank and our address in Germany, and other numbers, many numbers. Whatever! All that matters is that this paper is tangible proof of our departure! We climb into the trucks, the sick and convalescent watching, some in tears. Yes, a privileged 62 are leaving for home while tens of thousand others are still waiting, hoping. I try not to think about it.

In a station near Kharkov several freight car trains are parked. Ours is particularly long. The whole day was spent in putting it together. Trucks kept coming with prisoners from other camps. There were few guards. Who would have dreamed of escaping?

*

Fourteen amputees and twenty patients are in my car. No mattresses but enough space for sleeping. The car was clean. In the evening, an officer accompanied by six soldiers introduces himself. He is in charge of half of the train. He will be in the last car. The train will stop every day near a station and we can go out, take care of our needs, drink and eat bread. And the amputees? For us to deal with them. So much for the presentations. Looking outside I think we must be in the twentieth car of a train which has about fifty.

We could go down to stretch our legs on the tracks without danger. Prisoners and soldiers were distributing water for us to drink as much as we want and slices of black bread. We help the amputees to take care of their needs.

The train had not started yet. The Russian officer comes back. I introduce myself and we chat a bit:

191

- So you're a lieutenant, too. You were a prisoner of war with us?

- Yes, in the Donbass. And you, have you been in the war?

- No, I first finished my engineering studies and in May 1945 I joined my father's division near Frankfurt on the Oder. I stayed there a year to improve my German and my father found me this job accompanying released prisoners. This is my fifth convoy to Germany. The trip takes six to seven days. At Frankfurt-Oder you will stay fourteen days in quarantine, without leaving the train. You will be taken care of by the German health services. While waiting there I take the opportunity to see my father again before my return trip back in the other direction. Instead of prisoners I will be loaded with a lot of household items, clothing, food that I buy in the Red Army store to bring back to Kharkov. We also ship construction and hospital equipment, drugs, and everything else that is not avaible yet back home in the USSR. I am sure you have seen that so much is still lacking there.

- Yes, it's true.

- I already know that another transport of prisoners is waiting for me. Remember to close the door of the car at night. It's not that hot. And if the train stops for any reason do not go out without asking. Bandits and thieves are always around watching our trains.

- Thanks for the advice, lieutenant. One of your soldiers already warned me.

I felt relieved and confident, just happy. Nothing could stop me now and soon I will celebrate my return with my parents. I had forgotten too quickly that I was still in the land of the Soviets.

Our trip went as planned with a daily stop, unlimited water and three slices of bread. I shared the six slices that Irina had given me with an amputee who was suffering a lot on this umpteenth transport. Some were not to see the end of this trip. Two days before arriving in Germany three of them had died in my car, so close to their freedom! The officer told me to keep them with us in the car. They would be taken over by the German health service upon our arrival at the first German station. A certication would be issued that they had been released to their home country. I thought this was the ultimate hipocrisy.

- If there are any problems just tell the station master there. He is a major and a friend of mine. He speaks good German. Tell him you're a friend of Boris, that's my name.

*

On the seventh day of our journey our train stops on a siding about half a mile from the station. We are in Germany! It's still dark and rather cool outside. When the sun rises I open the door of the car. Some silhouettes appear in the morning mist, three uniformed men who speak German. I start to talk to them:

- You are German?

- Yes, but what are you doing out here? You are not allowed to leave your car. You are in quarantine for two weeks. Come on! Get back in the car immediately!

- There are four dead people in my car. I want the health department to come to remove them.

- Health department? What is that? And they leave, laughing like idiots.

Some distance from me a shot rang out. I run to see what was the matter. Two policemen aim their guns at one of sick from my car. What is going on ?

- Nothing, replied my friend, I saw this big pile of straw out there and I wanted to take some for the mattrasses of the amputees to make them a little more comfortable. Then these guys who say they are policemen called me a thief and asked for my papers, even threatening to send me back to Russia.

- Do not show them anything and return to the car.

Now I face five gunmen. Yes, the war is over but it has split Germany into occupation zones. Here the Red Army is in command. The five guys in front of me are German police, obviously appointed by the Soviets. I think that attack is the best defense and I demand to speak to their superior. First, how do they call their police?

- We are the 'People's Police' (nicknamed the infamous 'Vopos') and our boss is in command of this station.

- Ah, my friend the major is your commander?

- You know him ?

- Yes, go get him, right now.

Two of these guys run and soon come back with a third one. He is the major in charge of the Frankfurt-Oder station.

- I am a friend of Boris, a lieutenant like me.

- You know him?

- Yes, very well.

- What do you want?

- For starters, there are four dead people in my car and I guess some in other cars, too. Boris told me to get the health service to unload the bodies. Secondly, I would like to know who is responsible for our food. And finally I would like a bit of straw for our amputees. These poor guys have already suffered much.

- Negative for the straw. You are in quarantine, forbidden to get outside your car. For the rest, I take care of your people and your food.

I asked the policemen where they came from.

- We are all from Saxony.

- Well, that explains it!

Back in the car the young patient said he had been lucky to be saved by my intervention. I then asked if there were officers among them. One with an amputated leg answers:

- I was a major and I watched you during our transport and here. You know how to show your authority. How old are you ?

- 21, and you?

- 32. I was taken prisoner in 1944.

I took the floor:

- My dear comrades, we are stuck in this car for fourteen days. We'll have all the time to get to know each other. For now I'll take care of our four dead before they come to remove them.

I stood before the four dead bodies and I recited a long prayer. Barely finished with this ceremony the door opened and the police major and four men came and loaded the corpses onto a pickup truck.

- Comrade major, who takes care of our food?
- The Red Cross. They will come in no time.
- And what about our needs?
- Under the car, that's as far as you can go.
- It's very difficult for most of us. Could we not do it behind the straw?
- All right, granted.

At noon, the Red Cross came with an oatmeal soup and water, as much as we wanted. We would have the same menu for the entire quarantine.

The hours passed slowly. Boredom set in and with it came a lot of dark thoughts. We may as well enjoy that we are alive and use our ample time to tell our stories as I had suggested. One of the amputees asked me to start. As we had all the time in the world I started to talk about my youth, the war, my captivity and, of course, my Catholic faith. I actually finished my story on this topic with this question: "How many of you were brought up as believers?" Of thirty people there were three Catholics and four Protestant. "And how many remained faithful?" Two Catholics, including myself, none of the Protestants. Sad fact: Germany had already started losing its Christian soul between the wars. Nazism had only accelerated things.

I handed the floor over to one of the amputees. He was a major, 39, born in Leipzig. An only child, he attended university in this city:

"My father was a lawyer appointed Party Chief of the Saxony region in late 1942. I was drafted in 1943. After my officer training I left Germany in early 1944 with a tank unit in Greece. Wounded in a surprise attack I spent my convalescence in Leipzig with my parents. We had embraced the Nazi doctrines with enthusiasm. After several bombing of Leipzig and the irresistible advance of the Allied and with the 'secret weapons' of the Führer remaining invisible we stopped believing in the 'final victory'. When I got my marching orders to join a tank division in Russia my parents told me that the war was lost. All I could do was to try to come back safe and sound. But then, at the end of '44 our division was completely destroyed in the fighting on the central Eastern front. I lost a leg after an operation in a very primitive prisoner hospital. In two camps I received only a minuimum of care before arriving in our last hospital that was well equipped. And now with all of you I am on my way back to my homeland."

Someone else wants to 'exorcise' his past? I prompted another major to speak, a big guy, now minus an arm. He did not seem very eager but eventually he loosened his tongue, turning to me:

"I watched you in the hospital when you came with your team to transfer us to other barracks, then in the train and now here. You are very special. You have something extra. You are a believer. I have never prayed. I did not even know that prayer really existed. So I'll tell you about my life, all my life.

I was born in Berlin in 1919. My parents were communists, unemployed. We lived in a very small apartment in a rotten neighborhood. I slept with my sister in one room, my parents in another. We ate our meals in a tiny kitchen. Most of the time we had to tighten our belts with almost nothing to put in our mouths. My parents sent us to wealthier neighborhoods to pilfer food or snatch bags from old ladies. We were street children, real thugs. In 1930 my sister and I had seen a school from the outside. We could neither read nor write. My parents had gone to school before the first war and learned to read, write and count.

My father had fought in the 14-18 war. He was injured early in 1918. After his recovery he deserted the army and joined the Communist Party. Together with the anarchists they wanted to start the proletarian revolution. They were boycotting the production of ammunition, everything to hinder the German army. At the end of the war many soldiers and sailors joined them. The Communist Party became one of the major parties in Berlin.

We marched in the streets singing the 'Internationale'. But after the 1923 economic crisis, squalor settled in. The common workers in the large cities suffering enormously, no work and more and more unemployed.

Around 1930 my father heard of a movement, the "National-Socialist-German-Worker Party." Its leaders had promised to immediately give work to everyone once they would be in power. My father told my mother that he was going to learn more about it. One evening he came home quite late, a loaf of bread under his arm. He was happy to have met a former communist comrade who had become a member of the SA, the Nazis' private militia. He made an appointment for my father to meet his superior.

My father became a 100% 'National Socialist', a Nazi. In no time we were given a new apartment in a very nice neighborhood. My sister, who was three years older than I, had run away and no one was even looking for her. My father arranged for me to be admitted to a school run by uniformed SA teachers to learn to read and write. We were forty students, in school 8am to 6pm with a military-like iron discipline. Three years later I changed schools and I got into the National Socialist education system. In 1933 Hitler won just enough votes to be named Chancellor. My father became a hero among the SA. On the advice of a friend he asked to be admitted into the SS. In 1934 he was accepted and started with the ideological training specializing in 'Sonderkommando' work directly under Heinrich Himmler, the chief of the SS.

My parents now lived in a middle class neighborhood, in an apartment previously owned by a Jewish family who had been expelled by the SA. They even had a servant who also did the cooking. I saw my parents once a month and there was a lot to be surprised about. My father did not speak the same language as before and neither did my mother. They had radically changed their views. They now hobnobbed with the big bourgeoisie who had joined the Nazis and they proudly wore their Nazi insignia. Everyone around them said "Heil Hitler!" This had become their salvation. At the time I was proud of my father and of his success.

He was a tall, handsome man, strapping in his carefully tailored uniform, with a wide smile that made him so likable in the eyes of his newly found bourgeois friends. It was the facade. One day one of our Nazi educators told me that when my father was still with the SA he had cleared all our former suburban neighborhood of all the communists and anarchists and had them all arrested. They all were killed by SS 'Sonderkommandos', men, women and children, all shot to death. After that bulldozers had razed all their houses.

Silence.

- Your father had become a 'hero' of the new Germany.

No comment.

He went on: "I continued my studies, that is to say until the end of my Nazi indoctrination in '41. I enlisted in the army early in '42 in the infantry and became a lieutenant at the end of '42 after training at the war academy in Potsdam. I wrote to my parents but got no answer. I had three days before I had to ship out for my regiment. It was raining, therefore there was no air raid and I went to Berlin to see my parents. Arriving home, the building superintendent told me that my parents had moved a month ago. My father was appointed Party Chief of the region of Mecklenburg. I never heard from my parents again.

Our division had reached the center of Russia and after harsh battles I was injured in spring '43 and transported to a field hospital 60 miles behind the front. During my three weeks in the hospital I met the chief physician. He had a private clinic in the former Sudetenland, 15 miles from the German border. His clientele was mostly Czech, many of them in the resistance who could not be treated within Germany as the Gestapo and their collaborators had eyes everywhere. After the annexation of Czechoslovakia he continued to work in his clinic until end '42 when he had to go to Russia to head this field hospital.

One day the doctor asks me if I still believed in Hitler's victory. I answered no. He continued by asking me if I knew Reinhard Heydrich, chief of police and the Gestapo. I had heard about him. He had been much talked about in Berlin before Hitler's offensive against the Soviet Union. Well, that guy Heydrich was appointed by Hitler to be in charge of Czechoslovakia with unlimited powers. To better protect himself he had moved his command to a village near Prague. In short time, Heydrich became the most hated man in Czechoslovakia. The resistance plotted for his removal with the help of a commando from England that had parachuted into the area near Heydrich's headquarters. His assassination took place in front of Heydrich's entire staff. None of the commando survived and terrible reprisals happened in the aftermath. However, from that time on many of the worst SS Sonderkommando thugs became a lot more cautious and the bravery of the commandos may have saved many lives. That's what that senior doctor had said."

*

At long last the quarantine was over. During our last Red Cross meal the police major came over. In the afternoon, we were ready to write our name and address on a document that certified that we had spent two weeks in quarantine in Frankfurt-Oder. An hour later, we got out of our car that had been our confinement for so long and walked over to the station. The amputees were carried on stretchers and placed in waiting rooms. From a distance I saw Boris discussing something with another Russian officer. Instinctively, I wanted to wave him goodbye, but I chose not to. Okay, he had behaved decently towards me but it was better to avoid a potentially compromising gesture. So much for civility in the communist part of Germany!

Outside the station a civilian was talking into a microphone:

"You will travel in comfortable trains. Before boarding the train, the Red Cross will give you a slice of bread and water and you will receive a small bag of oat flakes as a gift. Those who go to the west into the American, British or French zones will find famine and disease and, according to the latest information, many have already died there." Pitching their propaganda to the last minute! No reaction among prisoners.

A train with real passenger cars was waiting for us! All was not wrong in this last phase of our going home: a slice of bread, lots of water and a pound of oatmeal, all provided by the Red Cross.

Eight of us per compartment. It was clean, all wood, I felt good. Night had long since fallen when the train finally started. I ate my slice of bread, drank and fell asleep until daybreak. Behind the window rain was falling in a steady stream as we passed one ruined city after another. I remembered Torsten, the SS-captain who lost all his family in October 1944 in the bombing of Leipzig.

My neighbor advised me not to go to the bathroom. Too disgusting! Even now there were still some soldiers who could not hold back their bowels. Nothing had changed in this respect: some of the former prisoners continued to void below the train at each stop.

*

And now for the connection to Hünfeld! A man in a white coat showed me where to go. We had to take the train to Eisenach, platform 4. I was walking fast in search of my train but my feet were terribly sore. The platform was overcrowded with former prisoners in their tattered Red Army rags. What a sinister carnival! A nurse from the Red Cross gave me a slice of bread with a thin layer of jam and a cup of hot coffee. She wanted to know my destination: Hünfeld near Fulda. "Ah! You're in luck, it's on the American side. A friend of mine with whom I worked in the last military hospital is now near Frankfurt am Main. We often write and so I am aware of what it is like there. Over here, we lack everything, especially food. Now hurry away to the first cars to find a seat."

I squeezed into a compartment in the middle of three former prisoners of war and five civilians. I looked at my feet. No wonder they hurt so bad! They were swollen, the skin taut as ready to split. Two civilians in front of me commented quietly. What were they saying? They spoke too low and, moreover, I did not care. I had only one desire: to leave the Soviet zone for good.

There still were controls. The first, just after the start and the second just before the arriving in the Eisenach station. The former prisoners were controlled by an officer and two soldiers of the Red Army who were demanding the release certificate. Civilians had to deal with their 'People's Police' who did not hesitate to rummage through their luggage. When they finally left, one of the civilians followed them. He had no luggage and did not have to show his papers. Ten minutes later I see him pass before our compartment. Where was he going? A police informant? A former Gestapo guy? They may simply have changed name!

Almost everywhere the ruins. I deciphered the station names flying by. They raised fleeting souvenirs. Eisenach. It was an evocative name, but of what? In my memory, too, but now just a lot of ruins. I had trouble concentrating. But of course! That was in 1938. Willy Unverzagt had organized a class trip to Eisenach. It was such a beautiful city, rich in history, with its museums, the castle and the park. All of us students were delighted with this excursion. Each of us had received a photo souvenir. A faint smile came to my lips at the thought of those happy times. So I was passing through this city. But what a contrast!

The Soviet officer showed up to once again check our papers while the 'People's Police' took all passengers who did not have tickets to the West out of the train including all civilians in our compartment except a woman. She asked me if I felt ok and I was touched by a little trite word when she addressed me. This word suddenly sounded so extraordinarily unusual to me, like something out of a long lost vocabulary. She had begun her sentence with "Sir".

Remaining one-to-one with her, I thanked her.

- Are you going to the American zone?

- Yes, to see my sister in Hanau, near Frankfurt. My husband had to stay back in Leipzig.

- But why ?
- That's the rule. You can never leave the Soviet zone. I have a special permission for three weeks. After that, back to Leipzig.
- Have you lived in Leipzig before the war?
- Yes, we both were born in Leipzig. My husband's factory was bombed in 1944. He built another one out of town and it is still running. Originally, we produced machine tools and now we are working for the Red Army. The entire production is shipped to the Soviet Union.
- Do the Russians pay you well?
- At delivery. You were prisoners of the Russians?
- Yes, since the end of the war.
- Then you must have suffered a lot. I saw your feet, full of water, and your face. You are like a skeleton.

The train suddenly slowed. We were at the east-west border. Nobody moved, but I recognized English voices just as in 1944 in Italy. The train left. Passing through the next station we saw American soldiers. Now we were really free! I wanted to jump for joy but I just had to sit down and I fell asleep until another prisoner shook me to show me the Americans! Tall fellows in well fitting uniforms. What a contrast with the 'Reds'! But I have again fallen asleep. I was really 'out'.

The train stops, a voice announces "Bad Hersfeld". My lady neighbor leaves. Now there are only three of us, three speechless former POWs.

- Are you not leaving here also?
- No. We are going to a camp for former prisoners.
- To do what ?
- Don't know. We'll see.

Go where you will. I was too tired to ask questions. The train stopped again and a voice called on all the prisoners to leave the train. I followed them like a robot. We were a sorry looking bunch of tired men evoking in me the old phrase of 'Lumpen-Proletariat.' Fatigue made me stagger a bit. One of the Americans had noticed. They took me to the first aid station. Ten prisoners were undressing.

One of the Americans in a white coat asked me in German: "Where did you come from?" I mumbled: "Donetsk region." Two men stretched out on a camp bed. The doctor saw my feet, took off my shoes and gave an order to a US military who returned with a tray and two glasses. I swallowed a rather thick sweet liquid. I already felt better but I still was as in a fog. "Rest while we take care of the others." The others. I saw them stark naked, emaciated, like puppets, but none of them had swollen feet. They had to repeat their names and the places where they had come from. Then they took these damn Red Army uniforms away.

He led me to another room. The doctor asked for my discharge papers. I pulled out my wallet. Did I have something else in the uniform? I shook my head, nothing.

- For now I will keep your wallet. You will take a shower. Your clothes go to disinfection. After that I will see you.

His two assistants helped me into the shower. They spoke German, but were they? "Yes, we are working here for the Americans. Come, we'll wash you because you are not able to stand up. It is rare that we have prisoners in as bad a state as you are." They soaped me, showered and rubbed me all over my body with a real towel before taking me back to the doctor. He checked me thoroughly and made me stand on a scale. Result: barely 100 pounds, with at least three pounds of it being the water in my feet and legs. One of the Germans helps me put back my 'memories of Russia.' With my Soviet cap and the red star I am the true image of a released prisoner! Putting on my shoes turned out to be impossible. "We will wrap your feet with strips of fabric. They will keep your feet warm." The doctor returned my wallet and my usual paraphernalia, my tin, my spoon and my little bag with oats, and the wire around my waist.

I was alone with the two Germans and the doctor:

- Normally our officers conduct a survey of each prisoner to determine the place of his captivity and his work but in your case we know you were in the Donetsk region. Here's a little food package as a gift from the US military. Your train to Hünfeld leaves in 45 minutes. My two nurses will come with you.

- You were a lieutenant?
- Yes, just when I was 20, heading an infantry company.
- See a doctor when you get home.

*

On the train, with my American package on my knees, I shared my compartment with two women and a young boy. For the first time, I was completely alone, without any fellow prisoner, just civilians around me. "Sir, where are you going?" wondered the boy. "Hünfeld coming up!" One of the two women slipped a few words to the boy and he stares at me without speaking.

I let myself drift into my thoughts. Quite unexpectedly I found myself in a very strange state. The hope to return left me cold, empty. I missed my comrades. Fatigue took over once more, I fell asleep. The child woke me up: "Sir, we are at Hünfeld."

Hünfeld! This station ... what memories! In the lobby of the train station I see faces that seemed familiar to me but without sharp edges, like in semi-consciousness. They were staring at me from all sides: "Another Russian who landed ..." But in those eyes I rather read "Poor guy".

Suddenly, a male voice calls out, "Are you Josef Pappert's brother?"

Yes, it's me. Two women came to me: "You? Aloÿs Pappert?" I nod. "We know you." A man pushes them back: "Leave him alone, don't you see he can hardly stand on his legs!"

He takes my US package and leads me to his taxi.

- You remember me? Josef Schwab, I have often driven you during the war.

I say nothing.

- I'll drive you your sister Klara's home.

No reaction.

When she saw me she took me in her arms, sobbing with joy. From my side, still nothing. I was cold. I shivered. Klara took me to the kitchen and sat me next to the stove. One might even say that she dropped me like a package and then left looking for Katherina. Maybe I had put my hands on the stove plate because when my sisters came back they rushed to remove them. My palms were burned. They were dismayed. "My God, my God, what a state you are in. Are you hurt?"

Silence.

- We'll make you something to eat."

Katherina first wanted to call Josef to come and get me, without telling my parents.

When Josef and I arrived at my parents, everyone, my mother, my father, Anna, Hedwig took me in their arms, everyone was crying for joy. My eyes were dry, I felt nothing. I was like a robot. They washed me, everyone wanted to touch me. My father said: "I told you, my son, to come back, even if only skin and bones. So he returned, but will he survive?"

Anna looked for trousers, a shirt and a sweater. We were all gathered around in the living room. My mother went to heat up the room but I still was shivering. They had me put on big slippers. We will prepare something to eat, my mother said.

- What do you want?

No answer.

Anna planted herself in front of me and repeated, "What do want you eat?" Finally I said "soup". My mother went to the kitchen:

- I'll make him a good soup with potatoes and a piece of butter.
- We do not know what he can eat.

Anna put the soup in front of me and gave me a spoon. I ate a little and asked for something to drink. Anna gave me water. I took it and said, I'm cold, I want to sleep.

Willy Unverzagt came by: "Philip, your son has returned, but he is a living death. We must ask your doctor to come tomorrow morning." My mother had already thought of this.

The next day, in the morning, my mother found me lying on the floor. Anna said, "You know, Mom, we know nothing about his prison life. For now we have to help him to regain consciousness." The doctor examined me and said there was nothing he could do: "He's in shock, in a terrible trauma but with patience you can get him out of it. Do not ask him to tell you about his prison experience. Better he should forget."

*

The third day I called my mother for my prisoner clothes. She had burned them. This provoked in me a feeling of panic, as if I had lost a part of myself.

I went back to bed. It was late afternoon. My mother and Anna tucked me in and I immediately sank into a deep sleep.

When my mother and Anna came to see me the next day they found me sitting on the bed: "Where am I?" My mother and Anna were taken aback: "You are at home with your parents, Anna, Josef and Hedwig."

Again, silence ... and suddenly I began to pray: "Holy Virgin, thank you for bringing me home." And as if all dykes had opened I could not stop my tears. My mother took me in her arms. She was happy. Anna ran downstairs to trumpet the good news: "He is risen! He got out of his nightmare!"

My father and Hedwig rushed into my room and held me in their arms. Everyone was in tears. Then Josef, Klara and Katherina arrived. Anna had already prepared breakfast and for the first time since my return I did not asked for a soup, but I drank coffee and ate heartily. "I'm so happy to be with you. I do not remember anything."

Josef had also phoned Willy Unverzagt and the doctor. They all came for lunch. Anna and Hedwig were in the kitchen. Josef had already passed the message that no one should asked me about my past. Everyone reveled in the joy of our reunion. The doctor quickly examined me and prescribed nothing but rest and told me to do everything possible to regain weight. Throughout the meal, I saw that everyone was happy.

After a few weeks I had gained some weight. My appetite had returned. Every day my father and I were taking a good walk avoiding as much as possible getting caught up in any conversation even with the people we knew.

The first Sunday of Advent my family took me to church. The church was packed. I saw many familiar faces but too many were missing. Like bodyguards, Josef and my father escorted me to avoid any encounters. For quite some time I just wanted to be alone. It took me quite a while before I became comfortable again to talk even to our friends. I knew that the day would come when I would be ready again to face my new life, my life after the war. But it would take a while.

It was Christmas 1946.

*

Post-Script

War stories abound, especially those about World War II - too many are about the lofty strategies of its generals or the infighting of the political leaders. Not enough of our war books show the suffering of the millions of men and women caused by the terrible consequences of their leaders's reckless ambitions.

Aloysius Pappert gives a gripping account of his ordeal in Stalin's horrendous prisoner of war camps, of barely surviving physically pain, starvation and the inhuman cruelty of his oppressors.

However, Aloysius Pappert's book is much more than just another story of what happened to so many prisoners of war. It is an elevating and moving account of suffering, redemption and the ultimate triumph of leadership - and of his Faith.

I was honored that my friend Pappert asked me to translate his French manuscript. Both of us knew that this would not be an easy task. It is not enough to find the equivalent words in another language. We also had to find ways to convey the emotions and the drama that are so well expressed in Pappert's original French writings. We wanted our readers to get the proper impression of the weight of Pappert's many traumatic experiences. Also, Pappert has his very own unique writing style that convincingly tells about dramatic situations in a way that the reader almost feels to be right there with the action.

Let the readers decide whether we succeeded in this lofty endeavor.

WOLFGANG MACK, PHD
SEATTLE, WASHINGTON, USA

Made in the USA
San Bernardino, CA
06 January 2017